VERY VINTAGE

THE GUIDE TO VINTAGE PATTERNS AND CLOTHING

black dog
publishing

london uk

FOREWORD

Without a doubt, ideas we have in the present are distilled from what we know of the past. However, these ideas only have significance if they reflect the time they are in. The term vintage describes clothing that has become synonymous with copy, literally mimicking design of the past, but the notion of vintage actually holds rich detailing and fabrics from previous eras which can intertwine with developing thoughts of today rather than stand alone as pastiche.

Boudicca has respect for the past in all areas of design, literature, art and poetry. All of these factors influence our working practice. For any designer it is, however, essential not to forget your own process and how your individual set of rules creates your ideas.

The Romantic Museum, for example, held the collectors of the past in awe and these libraries became our design reference at Boudicca. This came through, in the collection of the same name, in a montage of silhouette and fabrics but garments and ideas were treated more like a palimpsest—something that has been rewritten atop an artifact of the past.

One of the most important aspects of vintage and generating ideas is reiterated in Robert Rauschenberg's *Erased de Kooning*, 1953, which suggests that the power of any given idea is the relationship of the idea to the time within which it is created.

Brian Kirby and Zowie Broach of Boudicca.

WHAT IS VINTAGE?

For the purpose of this book all clothing of the twentieth century has been included under the umbrella term of vintage. Owing to the diverse world of vintage shopping and collecting others will understandably see more distinction between eras. Clothing before 1920 is often referred to as costume and whereas garments which were made after 1980 are referred to as retro. Whether it is Dior or Diesel, vintage fashion can be either a personal passion or a reference point for future trends.

Very Vintage: The Guide to Vintage Patterns and Clothing aims to chart changing twentieth century fashion against socio-economic and cultural movements. The focus is how fashion was created from these events and discoveries or produced as a reaction to them. Fashion cannot be looked at in isolation and should be viewed as a series of symbols which informs the viewer of our hopes, wants and desires and where we are positioned in relation to the current culture in which we inhabit. It is these reference points which make garments become true fashion and not some form of fancy dress. Whether we are dressed for the workplace, or part of a subculture, how we adorn ourselves says a great deal about who we are and how we view ourselves in relation to the rest of society.

Very Vintage is laid out in a chronological order but rather than merely noting every change in dress and silhouette over a particular period, each chapter focuses on the events which brought about fashion changes, putting them into context. The moments in history which have created dramatic changes in fashion are examined to allow a full understanding of fashion in relation to culture.

Looking back through history, the fashion of the time, the clothes people really wore and the labels *du jour,* are capable of reflecting the period they were produced in just as much as an interior or historical photograph. It is therefore important to bear in mind that a key piece may be very expensive—buying vintage is literally owning a piece of history. Some couture designers are seen as more than merely designers of clothing. They are high artists, such as Schiaparelli or Balenciaga, and their best work commands prices which you would expect to pay for an artwork of that magnitude. A general rule of thumb: if a garment was initially expensive it will most probably have retained its value due to the label and the craftsmanship involved in its production. A true couture piece usually takes 150 hours to produce which is understandably reflected in its price. Other factors which will have a significant bearing on price are genuine rarity or the garment being seen as an authentic item which has informed a current trend.

Some people enjoy vintage garments for their undeniable aesthetic value whereas others choose to purchase vintage as a future investment. Collector's pieces are usually not intended for wear and are often unwearable due to their size as well as age. Others collect vintage to add to their own current wardrobe and to experience the joy and delight of wearing something which is both unique and has its own history.

Finding hidden treasures ten, 20, 30 and 50 years old can be an exhilarating pastime as well as a costly one. Vintage treasures can be found in the melay of a jumble sale, the dark musty corners of a charity shop, a vintage specialist shop or auction. Once you start searching you can find vintage everywhere.

Iain Bromley and Dorota Wojciechowska.

Michael at Lachasse 1952.

Previous Page: Model wears Romantic Museum collection garment by Boudicca. Spring/Summer 2006.

A Norman Hartnell coat which typified the main silhouette of the 1950s. Hartnell was an English fashion designer appointed dressmaker to the British Royal Family in 1938. Image 1955.

1900–1930

*

THE INFLUENCE OF THE EXOTIC

Nancy Cunard, through her extravagant exotic jewellery, 1926, shows how the influence of Africa was adopted by high society. The English writer rejected her family's upper class values, devoting much of her life to fighting racism and fascism.

This chapter focuses on fashion at the turn of the century. From Japonism to the influence of Tutankhamen via the Ballets Russes, fashion at the dawn of the twentieth century is lavishly displayed. This chapter explains how society's evolution influenced fashion, not only in terms of overall silhouette, where waistlines and bodyshapes were nipped as a result of women's liberation, but also the major changes in the application of textiles and accessories.

HAUTE COUTURE

Haute couture had its first public appearance at the 1900 World Trade Fair in Paris. Although the number of designers showing at the fair was limited—Charles Frederick Worth, Jacques Doucet and Jeanne Pacquin to mention a few—the twentieth century could be called the century of the designer, especially in relation to fashion. No other century has recorded or given such acclaim to those responsible for the creations of style. Designers prevailed in the era, unlike the previous centuries where Western clothing was predominantly court led and identifiable with the current ruler— Elizabethan, Regency and Victorian are well-known examples. Ever since designer, Charles Frederick Worth, first signed his dresses in the late nineteenth century the public has paid homage and feted designers, claiming them to be geniuses and artists. Twentieth century fashion has changed more quickly than at any other period in history and we, as consumers, at some level are able to be part of this arena. Cut free from court fashion, where ideas evolved and matured slowly often over a monarch's reign, fashion now appears as in a blur, with an ever-changing kaleidoscope of silhouette and reference points, as designers strive to give us as many as four collections a year along with their diffusion lines.

For it to be attractive, and ultimately purchased, this clothing must speak to us and about our aspirations and current lifestyles as well as be aesthetically pleasing.

Throughout history court fashion knew its place and the people new theirs. Sumptuary laws were introduced in the Middle Ages and lasted till the end of the Renaissance period, helping to establish clear divides between the classes. The use of certain fabrics, colours (purple being a signifier of expense) and trimmings (such as silk or fur) or the extravagant use of jewels, would inform the world of a person's class and position. The high fashions were introduced by the social elite and gradually filtered down to the lower classes. With fashion moving away from court dress and the decline in the European monarchy itself, how fashion is read and perceived has become far more complex. High fashion and its pinnacle, couture, are notably not interested in the everyday, the average or commonplace.

Portrait of Sir Walter Raleigh,
1585, and a Lady of the Royal
Austrian Court, 1578, representing
the court fashion as it was dictated
to the public.

Opposite: Erte (aka Romain de Tirtoff) fashion illustration, circa 1920.

The extravagant dress for a bride, depicting 1920s glamour in its full splendor, 1929.

CHARLES FREDERICK WORTH

British courier, Charles Frederick Worth, with his first collection
in 1865, was the first person to pioneer fashion as we know it. Not
content with merely supplying the Empress Eugene with gowns
when he opened the first fashion house in 1858 in the Rue de la Paix,
Paris, Worth had started the wheel of fashion that is evident today.
As Worth presented one annual collection he created the notion of
being *in fashion*; of fashion moving through phases and the ideology
of certain looks being in and, just as quickly, out. The designers at
the turn of the century, now free of court rules and regulations
with an ever widening client base, had to look elsewhere for
inspiration. Although fashion was free of the constraints of court
etiquette, members of the court and royalty were still influential
in promoting looks and defining what was acceptable in society as
a whole. The wife of King Edward VII, Queen Alexandra, was the
leader of society fashion for the upper and middle classes in the
late Victorian, early Edwardian, period. Alexandra depicted high
fashion through specific expensive adornments—her pearl chokers
and borzoi dogs. The fashion influence of the English court and
aristocracy was felt throughout the century, from (turn-of-the-
century) Queen Alexandra to Princess Margaret in the 1960s and
finally Diana Princess of Wales in the latter part of the century.

The desire to be current can be seen in the rapid 1860s expanse of designer Worth's fashion empire. When he originally opened his atelier, Worth employed just 20 staff. Less than ten years later, in 1868, the atelier had a staff of 1,200 catering for the needs of women at the top end of society. Early garments that could actually be called true fashion—ie. not court fashion—were not available to everybody and were exclusive to the upper classes. It was not until the 1860s that fashion became something which women of all classes could participate in.

Opposite and Right: Two of the extravagant and pioneering Charles Frederick Worth dress from the early 1900s.

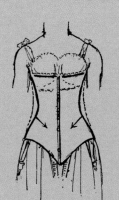

Far Left: A diagram depicting the corset and its effect in creating the 'S' bodyshape for a woman.

Left: The corset in action, accentuating hips and cleavage, circa 1950.

Opposite: Camille Clifford was the physical realisation of the Gibson Girl who referenced the feminine 'S' shape in popular illustration during the Edwardian era.

Charles Frederick Worth did not reform the design of female dress *per se*. The corset had defined female silhouettes throughout history thus far and Worth retained this corseted shape in his designs. He did, however, change the crinoline for the bustle. Crinoline was the rigid fabric used to stiffen the petticoat or rigid skirt-shaped structure of steel which supported the skirts of a woman's dress. It was Worth who morphed these elements so that the original fullness of the skirt was moved to the back of the body and floated over a wire cage at the rear. This moved the silhouette into an 'S' shape. If viewed from the side, the female form had become an 'S' with a large monobosom at the front to balance out the extended rear created by the bussle. This figure was to prove popular in the late Victorian period and well into the Edwardian era.

The most famous icon of the 'S' shape was not a real woman but in fact, an illustration, named the Gibson Girl, created by Charles Dane. Appearing in *Colliers* magazine from 1890–1910, the Gibson Girl's idealised figure was made flesh by Camille Clifford and was a forerunner to the modern day pin-up.

The 'S' shape found favour in all levels of society. The overt sexuality and fetishistic overtone which is currently attached to the corseted female form was not the view held by society at the beginning of the twentieth century. In fact, the corseted form was adopted by respectable women and viewed as the normal dress for decent members of society. Despite its aesthetic appeal there were issues with the practicality of Worth's redesign of the female bodyshape. The 'S' shape was still as restrictive for women as the original corset. The dress reform, which freed women from these restrictions and gave a more natural figure, was never pioneered by the couture houses of fashion at the time. This eventual change was due to a variety of socio-economic and cultural changes.

DRESS REFORM

The reform of dress, alongside women getting the vote, occurred more quickly in other countries, rather than in America or Europe. New Zealand was the first country to give women the vote and dress reform was originally seen there. Amelia Bloomer, an American whose name is forever associated with women's underclothes, was not in fact the inventor of the bloomer—a misconception of her namesake. As opposed to a designer, Bloomer was a pioneer of bloomers as a form of dress. By adopting this freer style, Bloomer was able to give herself greater mobility in accordance to the rising hemlines. This radical change in female dress did not outrage other women in society, however, several men saw this reworking of female fashion as degenerate and a challenge to their masculinity and thereby their authority.

Through the arts in England, notably the aesthetic movement, the struggle for female equality was pioneered. The rise of women's suffrage had gathered support towards the end of the nineteenth century and would be a constant battle until the end of the First World War when women over 30 years of age were given the vote as acknowledgement of female effort in the conflict. The aesthetic movement can be viewed as the British version of French symbolism and flourished in England from the 1860s until the beginning of the twentieth century. The trial of Oscar Wilde, a leading aesthete, can be seen as the end of the movement in 1901. The aesthetes believed in the pure beauty of art, coining the mantra: "art for art's sake".

Opposite: The reclaiming of the bloomer, pioneered by American, Amelia Bloomer, circa 1910.

Oscar Wilde, 1854–1900. As a leading aesthete, Wilde was one of the most successful playwrights of late Victorian London.

An example of the Japonism fashion worn by a model, circa 1920.

Opposite Top: An antique William Morris design, circa 1915. Morris was influential in the resurgence of traditional textile arts in the wake of the industrial revolution.

Opposite Bottom: Christopher Dresser teapot.

simplicity of line, often made from sensuous fabrics such as liberty silk, silk velvet or wool. The other style of dress popular with the movement was inspired by traditional Japanese dress.

Japan, as a country and a culture, was a relatively new discovery to the West in the early stages of the twentieth century. The influence of Japan on Western culture cannot be underestimated at this time. It was Japanese woodblock prints that influenced the members of the Impressionist movement and especially Post-Impressionists such as Vincent Van Gogh.[1] In Britain numerous artists as designers were influenced by Japanese culture and design, namely Christopher Dresser, James McNeill Whistler and Aubrey Beardsley. In fact Whistler and Beardsley were so influenced by Japanese art that their visual composition and personal signatures became very Japanese in style. The Japanese influence on dress can be clearly seen in Whistler's portraits, especially *Symphony in White No. 1*, 1862, where the female figure holds a Japanese fan as an accessory whilst residing in a room with aesthetic movement sensibilities—a lavish display of blue and white porcelain. A further example is *La Princesse du Pays de la Porcelaine (The Princess from the Land of Porcelain)*, 1878, a portrait housed in Whistler's famous Peacock Room, the Japanese-styled dining room

[1] Impressionism was an art movement that was championed largely by painters. Characteristics of Impressionist painting include visible brushstrokes, emphasis on light in its changing qualities, ordinary subject matter, the inclusion of movement and unusual visual angles.

Within the movement art was cut free from ideas of narrative, morals or practical considerations and existed purely as a feast for the senses. One of the main influences on the aesthetic movement was Japan, or Japonism as the style was referred to at the time. Japonism did not only affect dress but had a strong influence on the artistic and literary set of the day. Their homes were decorated with blue and white porcelain, ebonised furniture and a design ethic which was prominently influenced by nature, albeit the exotic, such as the placing of peacock feathers in a vase rather than flowers. The aesthetic movement can be seen to have links with the Pre-Raphaelites but rejected the movement's moral and social goals. The aesthetic movement's belief that the arts should provide a direct sensuous pleasure conflicted with the reverence for simplicity and handiwork sought by William Morris and the other Pre-Raphaelites.

Aesthetic dress of the 1880s to 1890s had many similarities to the artistic dress worn by the Pre-Raphaelites. At first glance there can be seen a rejection of the tightlacing and bustle that was popular in society. Aesthetic dress was cut looser in a more medieval-influenced style. The garments were loose fitting gowns designed with

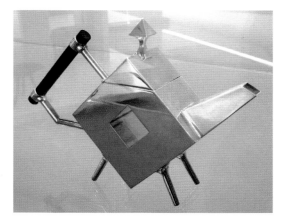

in the London home of Frederick R Leyland, which is an excellent example of the aesthetic movement in people's homes. The figure in *La Princesse du Pays de la Porcelaine* is clearly elongated which is very reminiscent of Japanese figure drawing and is depicted wearing a kimono in an aesthetically-themed drawing room. This style of dress would not have been worn in respectable society and was initially adopted only by those in artistic circles. It was from these circles that the dress of the aesthetic protagonists was adopted by the intellectual middle classes. This style of dress gave rise to the lightly corseted tea gowns of the early twentieth century, which in turn paved the way for the exotic creations of Paul Poiret.

The East, if not solely the Orient, was to inspire the Edwardian era until the outbreak of the First World War in 1914. Icons of the period appeared with their Borzoi dogs, a symbol of Imperial Russia made popular in England by Queen Alexandria. Such icons included Sarah Bernhardt, Isadora Duncan, Mata Hari and Lois Fuller who mainly came from the world of theatre and performance.

Inspiration for the time's icons often had historical reference points and included Cleopatra and Madame Du Barry. These women symbolised the female as predator, not prey, who used her charms to gain power over men. This idea of the *femme fatale* was common in the arts of the period, including an earlier reference in the painting *The Heart of the Rose*, 1889, by Sir Edward Coley Burne-Jones. The female form as an exotic creature can be seen in the prevailing European design movement of the time, art nouveau, which often used the dancer Lois Fuller and the actress Sarah Bernhardt as reference points. This can be clearly seen in the illustrations by Alphonse Mucha and the adornments made for Bernhardt by famous art nouveau jeweller, René Lalique. The female form, free from the restrictions of the corset and other structured clothing, can be viewed as their inspiration.

The end of the decade also gave rise to the most stylish event of the beginning of the twentieth century—Black Ascot. Edward VII had died in 1910, shortly before a racing event at Ascot. As a mark of respect to this much loved monarch who enjoyed sports and the good life, high society turned out in mourning dress for the event. Black Ascot itself was the inspiration for the Ascot scene in *My Fair Lady,* 1964. It was Cecil Beaton who designed the sets and costume for the film which won him the 1964 Oscar for his costume design. Beaton was an image maker, predominantly working in photography, who looked to the *Belle Époque* for inspiration in his work.[2] During his lengthy career Beaton worked on many films, from the infamous *My Fair Lady* to *Gigi*, 1958, and depicted Queen Elizabeth as a Winterhalter fairytale. Cecil Beaton's imagery is one of the most accessible ways for us to connect with this period and to get a feel of the luxurious and leisured lifestyle that was initially lost after the First World War.

[2] Occurring during the French Third Republic and the German Empire, the *Belle Époque* was considered a golden age, as peace prevailed between the major powers of Europe and was seen as the period of settled and comfortable life preceding the First World War.

Opposite: The Peacock Skirt, illustration by Aubrey Beardsley for Oscar Wilde's play *Salomé: A Tragedy in One Act*, 1893

Isadora Duncan, 1877–1927, was a dancer, considered by some to be the mother of modern dance and is one of the key fashion icons of the period.

PAUL POIRET

After Worth, Paul Poiret is the designer most frequently mentioned for changing the female silhouette and constructing the world of couture that is now so familiar in the present day. It was Poiret who made the first designer fragrance, Rose de Rosine, named after his daughter. This was a decade before Coco Chanel gave us her timeless fragrance, Chanel No 5. Poiret was the fist designer to open a lifestyle boutique, selling fabrics and furnishings to an upmarket clientele. During his career Poiret had worked for a number of other fashion houses to build his empire. Primarily he worked for fashion designer, Jacques Doucet, as an umbrella delivery boy, followed by two years at the Worth atelier. Following this, in 1903 Poiret, financed by his mother, opened his own small studio specialising in the redesign of the female silhouette. By 1906, he was a star.

Opposite Top: Paul Poiret, circa 1913. Poiret's contributions to twentieth century fashion have been likened to Pablo Picasso's contributions to art.

Opposite Bottom: One of Poiret's models shows the clothing inspired by the exotic cultures, which defined the fashion of the period. Especially indicative of this Eastern influence are the spacious harem pants, 1914.

Top and Bottom: A selection of the Paul Poiret looks from 1914.

Poiret claimed to have waged war on the corset and brought a more realistic shape to fashion: the *directoire* style. This style is where the skirt starts from just under the bust and falls sheath-like to the floor. In conjunction with the *directoire* style, one of the most notable contributions that Poiret made was the introduction of the East as a source of ideas. Fashion inspiration was no longer confined to Japan, which had stimulated creativity in earlier decades, and Poiret's look was motivated by the Middle East. He created harem pants and turbans trimmed with exotic feathers for the *demimonde* to be seen in on the Champs Elyse.[3] Ironically, Poiret himself had never travelled to the East and his inspiration came from an exhibition of Persian carpets he had seen in a French department store. Another source of inspiration could have been the Ballets Russes (Russian Ballet). Although he never openly cited their influence, it was after the ballet's arrival and subsequent success in Paris in 1909 that Poiret's work began to be more elaborate and make greater reference to other cultures.

[3] *Demimonde* was a polite nineteenth century term that was often used in the same way that 'mistress' is used today.

FASHION IS NOT SOMETHING
WHICH ONLY EXISTS IN DRESSES.
FASHION IS IN THE SKY, IN THE
STREET, IN THE WAY WE LIVE.

COCO CHANEL

THE BALLETS RUSSES

In the present day and age it is hard to imagine what a large impact a ballet company could have had on contemporary society. However, the Ballets Russes impacted on all aspects of culture in the early part of the twentieth century. The Ballets Russes, with their previously unseen pale pastel shades, brought an overnight, thunderbolt end to Edwardian fashion. Under the directorship of Serge Diaghilev the Ballets Russes opened in Paris in 1909 and in London in 1910. The Ballets both shocked and enthralled society with pioneering works such as *L'arpres-midi d'un Faune*, 1912, and *The Rite of Spring*, 1913. It was with the costumes and themes for the Ballets Russes that inspired and influenced the fashion of the time. The principal costume designer on the early ballets was Leon Baskt and it was his costumes for the ballets *The Firebird*, 1910, *Scheherazade*, 1910, *Le Spectre de la Rose*, 1912, and *Daphnis and Chloe*, and *Le Dieu Bleu*, both in 1912, which initially introduced the exotic to Western audiences of the time. The ballet *Le Dieu Bleu (The Blue God)*, although a commercial disaster for the director, Diaghilev, was the most influential on fashion in the period. The ballet made reference to exotic Siamese dance and the costumes were influenced by Eastern sensibilities.

The Ballets Russes attracted a great deal of attention during its 20 year span—1909–1929—not only from the public but also from artists and designers of the period. In later decades of the century and right up until present day designers have sought inspiration from the extravagant group. During the ballet's existence artists such as Pablo Picasso, Henri Matisse and Salvador Dalí produced their costumes. Coco Chanel was also involved but no designers were as influential on the public as the very early Ballets Russes costumes by Leon Baskt. It is the costumes by Baskt, with early principal dancers Vaslav Nijinsky and Anna Pavlova, that have continued to inspire fashion designers today. Yves Saint Laurent's Ballets Russes collection, 1976, is a notable example and, more recently, the influence of the Ballets Russes can be seen in John Galliano's work for the Dior fashion house. The Ballets Russes looks set to influence fashion once more when the Victoria & Albert Museum, London, launch a major retrospective of the company in 2010.

Previous Page: Paul Poiret illustration depicting a kimono style gown, circa 1912. Poiret has cleverly moved the main detailing of the piece to the back of the figure creating a streamlined shape.

Opposite: Vaslav Nijinsky was a Russian ballet dancer and choreographer. As one of the most gifted male dancers in history he was celebrated for his virtuosity and for the depth and intensity of his characterisations.

Top: Two of the dancers for the Ballets Russes, circa 1911. The Ballets was established in 1909 by the Russian impresario Serge Diaghilev. The influences of the Ballets' style was felt throughout society in the early 1900s.

THE FIRST WORLD WAR

The First World War, 1914–1918, changed society forever. The pre-existing social order, which had existed for centuries, was swept away during the war, as mainland Europe was reshaped and countries deposed their crowned heads of state and replaced them with elected democracies. This change was to have a profound effect on fashion and the world that belonged to Paul Poiret was gone forever. With both men and women pitching in for the war effort the roles of women in society were also changing. From previously being seen by the upper classes as merely decorative creatures situated below men, women had entered the world of work. Through the labour shortage during the war there was a necessity for women to work shoulder to shoulder with men, giving many their first taste of economic freedom.

Social order changed irrevocably after the First World War and the clientele for couture houses changed with it. No longer was there such an obvious distinction between social classes. The high class female aristocracy, the wife of an industrialist and the *demimonde* would become identical. Paris saw an influx of the *nouveau riche* (new rich) during this period as dollar-laden Americans filled the city. These deposed heads of state and idle rich were to become members of cafe society—world citizens belonging to nowhere and yet at home in every fashionable playground there was, be it London, Paris, Venice or New York. The world between the wars saw Paris filled with the likes of Barbara Hutton and Doris Duke (who were dubbed the Gold Dust Twins by the press due to their vast fortunes) who had come to Europe to find husbands—preferably with titles.

In this climate new designers appeared and new icons replaced the ones of the previous decade. Designers who enjoyed success at the time included Coco Chanel, who had launched a boutique selling designer sportswear just before the First World War in 1913. By 1919 Chanel had opened a showroom in the Rue Cambon, Paris, where her relaxed designs were addressing the needs of the modern woman. Chanel pioneered silk jersey, a fabric which had only ever been used for underwear and was attractive in its alternativeness to her upper class clientele.

Despite the boom in the fashion industry between the wars Paul Poiret never regained his position of prominence. In an industry where designers like Chanel were producing simple, sleek clothes that relied on excellent workmanship, Poiret could not compete. The designer who had given woman the modern day bra and flesh coloured stockings could not adapt to the changing times and was to die penniless after numerous unsuccessful attempts to reclaim his position in the world of couture fashion.

Opposite: One of the many zepplins used in the First World War, circa 1915.

Landgirl, 1916. A member of the Women's Land Army in the First World War. Photograph by F J Mortimer.

A dashing example of the popular bob haircut, circa 1925.

Opposite: Actress Carmel Myers displays the 1920s silhouette and the infamous Eton crop hairstyle.

The 1920s was a period of great social change and which reflected in art movements of the time such as Dada, 1916–1923, which was focussed on chaos and chance happening. Dada was a reaction to a world in which people now lived that appeared to have been turned upside down. Society's youth were now the leaders in fashion and style, a position they still hold today. The youth of the time were interested in being daring and trying everything new—dances, music, fashion, places to go and be seen.

During the 1920s, as a mark of their newfound freedom, women cut their hair. The previous style had been a bob and, later, would become even shorter with the Eton crop, which in turn brought about the invention of the drop earring (as ear lobes were now exposed). The suntan, the little black dress and nail varnish were all introduced and glamorised by Coco Chanel at this time. Chanel's use of outsized costume jewellery seemed to fit the period perfectly and the cultural icons are still relevant in today's society—think of Victoria Beckham without a suntan, nail varnish or little black dress.

THE EXOTIC
INFLUENCE

Opposite: Entertainer Josephine Baker in banana skirt from the Folies Bergère production *Un Vent de Folie*, 1927. After becoming a French citizen in 1937 Baker became a noted singer and celebrated dancer. Given the nickname 'Black Venus', Baker was the embodiment of the celebration of African influence in the early 1900s.

Left: Zandra Rhodes is one of the many designers who has utilised the turn of the century African influence in more modern times. This image displays vast quantities of African-inspired imagery. Photograph by Robyn Beeche. Image courtesy Zandra Rhodes.

Right: Marjorie Merriweather Post, circa 1930. Post was an American socialite. She was one of the exceptional women who remained unaffected by the Wall Street crash.

In the 1920s there was a renewed interest in the African continent which took many forms. In the late nineteenth and early twentieth century the French were expanding their empire, notably in Africa and African artefacts, and stories of the exotic continent filled the press. This, in turn, influenced artists, most notably Picasso, whose black period, 1907–1909, made direct reference to the tribal art of the continent. This African influence can be seen in his painting *Les Demoiselles d'Avignon*, 1907, and later cubist works. By the 1920s African rhythms were also influencing popular music of the time. Jazz music and revues such as the *Revue Negre*, 1926, were to have a major impact on fashion and popular culture. Performer Josephine Baker, 1906–1975, appeared to be the living embodiment of the African continent with her freeform dance moves and near nudity. The notion of black beauty would not be as highly praised for almost another 40 years. The youth revolution of the 1960s complimented black beauty and it was championed in fashion by highly esteemed designer Yves Saint Laurent. The appearance of Donyale Luna, one of the first notable African American supermodels, on the cover of *Vogue*, March 1966, was proof that black beauty had received recognition from mainstream Western audiences.

Black Africa was a source of inspiration for many of the avant garde in the 1930s. High society heiress, Nancy Cunard, is largely remembered for her love of African jewellery as she often wore tribal bangles up to her elbows on both arms and with her heavily kohled eyes—high fashion's interpretation of the African continent's influences. Black Africa has been a source of inspiration for avant garde designers in the late twentieth century. Designers such as Yves Saint Laurent and Zandra Rhodes were influenced in the late 1960s and 1970s respectively.

An archaeological discovery made in northern Africa in the 1920s was to have profound effect on Western art, most notably in the decorative arts, fashion and architecture. In Egypt tomb of the boy pharaoh, Tutankhamen, was discovered in 1922 by Howard Carter. The contents of the tomb would bring about a renewed interest in the ancient Egypt and would influence the decade. The strong geometric patterns and bold use of flat colour found in the tomb became key elements in the massive art deco movement.

The 1929 Wall Street Crash (or Crash of 29), the colossal implosion of the stock market, marked the end of the 1920s and brought about a shift in fashion. The short skirts which had symbolised the prosperity and economic boom of the decade were to skim the floor as recession had an effect on the lives of many. The warmer, floor-grazing skirt was a functional rather than fashionable choice. Those members of society that were less effected by the recession revelled in luxury, showing the world that they were still prosperous and able to ride out the economic crisis.

Top Left and Right: Here is an exquisite kimono and pattern from the 1920s. This look was popular as the exotic East influenced Western fashion. The pattern pieces opposite depicted create a longer shape than in the image but the basic shape is the same.

THE BASIC KIMONO

① Basic Kimono

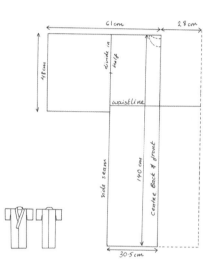

- 61 cm
- 28 cm
- 48 cm
- double in height
- waistline
- side seam
- 140 cm
- Centre Back & front
- 30.5 cm

②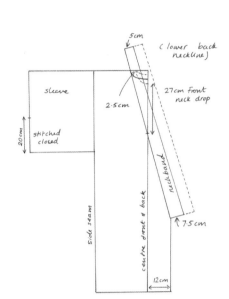

- 5 cm
- (lower back neckline)
- sleeve
- stitched closed
- 20 cm
- 2.5 cm
- 27 cm front neck drop
- neckband
- side seam
- centre front & back
- 7.5 cm
- 12 cm

③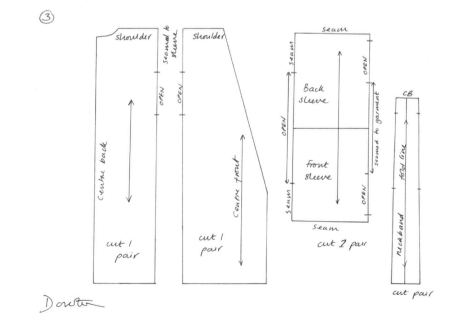

- shoulder
- seamed to sleeve
- shoulder
- OPEN
- OPEN
- Centre back
- Centre front
- cut 1 pair
- cut 1 pair
- seam
- seam
- OPEN
- Back sleeve
- OPEN
- seamed to garment
- Front sleeve
- OPEN
- seam
- seam
- cut 2 pair
- CB
- neckband
- fold line
- cut pair

Dorota

THIS BASIC KIMONO SHAPE IS BASED ON TRADITIONAL DESIGN. THE PATTERN CAN EASILY BE ADAPTED BY ADDING POCKETS AND TRIMMINGS. ILLUSTRATION BY DOROTA WOJCIECHOWSKA.

1930—1940

*

THE MAGIC
OF
HOLLYWOOD

The stunning Grace Kelly, circa 1955. In 1952 Kelly obtained the role of Linda Nordley in MGM's *Mogambo* and so began an illustrious film career. This film helped to establish Kelly as an icon of the time.

Having been part of the fashion climate for some time the defining stars of the 1930s era, in collaboration with the costume designers of the Hollywood studio system, sold high fashion and a sense of narrative mystique to the masses. The golden age of Hollywood has had a direct impact on fashion today and has its roots in 1930s culture. This chapter explores the public's use of paper patterns in their own homes to interpret the high fashion that was represented to them at the time.

HOLLYWOOD

In today's society, Hollywood is a vehicle for design houses to showcase their couture creations. These dresses are worn by top film stars down the red carpet to the legendary Academy Awards ceremony. These couture pieces are complimented by expensive borrowed jewels as the ceremony is watched by millions of people. Fashion and film have gone hand in hand for the best part of a century since the Hollywood studios used the former as a marketing tool in the 1930s to attract women audiences into cinemas. Indeed the whole concept of shopping for vintage can be viewed as being created by Hollywood in 1967 when Faye Dunanway appeared in 1930s attire for her role as the female lead in *Bonnie and Clyde*, 1967. This film created nostalgia for the past and the idea of thrift shop fashion, literally reclaiming garments from a bygone era, became desirable amongst the general public. Before the 1960s and the release of the film, the only people to wear secondhand clothing were the economically challenged, but with the release of the film, and the following public interest surrounding the 1930s, dubbed art deco, the notion of shopping for vintage and putting an individual look together was born.

At the beginning of the twentieth century America saw a large number of immigrants arrive on its shores, especially from Europe. The reasons for this influx were many and varied—from those fleeing persecution (the Jews of Imperial Russia), to those who wanted to own land which, back in Europe, which was usually the preserve of the rich and titled. The cinema allowed all these people to see a (somewhat fantastical) version of what it was to be American, to live the modern lifestyle and to belong to the new century.

For women, cinema was an ideal vehicle which allowed them to learn how to reinvent themselves and to be current. In the dark and isolation of the cinema, where the viewer is in sole communion with the star on the screen, it is very easy to project personal wants and desires onto the seemingly unattainable icon and, in turn, want to emulate the stars' obviously dramatised but nonetheless appealing qualities.

Film was originally seen as situated slightly above sideshow entertainment from its conception in 1895. Actors, who saw their voices as a major part of their craft, did not want to be named in these early silent showreels and were often described in the credits as, 'man with bicycle' or 'woman with hat'. By 1907 there were over 4,000 Nickelodeon cinemas throughout America. The industry was changing and growing rapidly and, in 1915, DW Griffith had made the iconic film *Birth of a Nation* starring Lillian Gish. Gish was one of the first international stars of cinema and a role model for many women during the war. Legions of women left behind the Poiret-created ideology of the female as an exotic creature and would pose like the seemingly innocent and girly Gish for photographs sent to

their loved ones on the frontline. It is an interesting fact that, unlike today, the early Hollywood system was dominated by women. It was women who opened films and were the real earners in this new media. Stars such as Alla Nazimova, Pola Negri, Lillian Gish and Mary Pickford were the real power players of 1920s American cinema.

Hollywood grew up in the orange groves that surrounded Los Angeles. At the beginning of the twentieth century this land was cheap to buy and sunlight was plentiful, attracting film makers. By 1918 the open lot was replaced with the blacked-out studios. The controlled lighting meant shooting could continue both night and day as the actors were lit by floodlights and could be separated from the background in a more controlled and clear manor. America was not the only country to have a thriving cinema at the beginning of the century. France and Italy were the most popular types of cinema but, due to the catastrophic events that unfolded in Europe during the First World War, Hollywood was able to take the lead position it has maintained ever since.

Hollywood, at the beginning of the 1920s, saw two major changes: the introduction of the star system and the organisation of the studio system. There were eight studios in Hollywood by the 1930s, the top five being Metro Goldwyn Meyer (MGM), Twentieth Century Fox, Paramount, RKO Pictures and United Artists. Each studio released an average of one film each a week—a total of 260 feature films a year. The productions of the other three studios meant that there were over 400 films being released annually. At this time the star system was binding contracts between the studio and actor. For an actor in the silent film period their main selling point was their looks and within these studio contracts there were strict guidelines which told the star how to behave both on and off screen. Female stars were required to be well dressed and in full makeup at all times. Male actors were contractually obliged to act like perfect gentlemen, reiterating the moral guidelines of the era. For all stars there were morality clauses as the studios had often invested heavily in both time and money in creating the star, albeit an idealised version. New identities, backgrounds and names were given to these stars in order for them to fulfill the public's yearning and expectations.

PAPER PATTERNS

By the 1930s studios were using fashion as a marketing tool to attract women to the cinema and giving fashion advice and tips to the audience through movie magazines such as *Photoplay, Silver Screen* and *Movie Mirror*. Such was the public's demand to look like the stars that both *Silver Screen* and *Movie Mirror* advertised clothing patterns based on a particular star's latest film. Film magazines were not the only companies to produce patterns for the home market. The company Butterick launched Starred Patterns which featured glamour outfits similar to those worn by the prevalent stars.

The importance of the patterns which were available to the home dressmaker cannot be underplayed. Before the 1970s, and the dominance of the high street with its retail chainstores, paper patterns produced by companies such as Vogue, Butterick, McCalls and Style Simplicity were often the only way that many women could obtain the latest high fashion looks and style. The paper pattern market was not just a large part of women lives in America and in Britain, but also in commonwealth countries where expats would want to retain some vestige of contact with their mother country. These patterns were fundamental in keeping women in countries such as New Zealand and Australia in touch with European fashions and trends. Vogue (not associated with the magazine of the same name) and other pattern producing companies would often have licence deals with couturiers and design houses such as Bellville Sassoon. The companies would buy directly from the designer after seeing the collections and make these designs available to women worldwide. As a purchasable item, the pattern envelope would feature a designer's name and the designer would supply the company with an actual finished garment, a *toile* (calico mock up) and a paper pattern. The pattern which was sold to the consumer was simplified so it could be more easily assembled at home, although the photograph on the cover would be of he original dress supplied by the designer.

Some idea of the size of the paper pattern market can be gleaned for the fact that companies such as Style Simplicity would produce thirty new patterns every month. Styles which sold well would be kept in the book for up to five years and less popular styles would be pulled form the inventory very quickly. In a way, these patterns allowed all women to wear couture: the dressmaker may have been your own mother but it was a bespoke handmade outfit created especially for you.

COSMETICS

American cinema also introduced the modern woman to cosmetics which had been previously frowned upon and seen as only for those with loose morals. The present day brand, Max Factor, was also the name on makeup used by the stars of the time. The company was founded in 1907 by Polish immigrant Factor. Previously Factor had worked as a makeup artist for the Imperial Russian Ballet. He opened a beauty salon on Hollywood Boulevard and his clients included the cream of Hollywood during the 1920s and 30s—Jean Harlow, Claudette Colbert, Bette Davis, Norma Shearer, Joan Crawford and Judy Garland were all regular clients. Factor even helped Clara Bow, the original 'it girl', define her look by giving her the heart shaped lips which would become her visual trademark. During the 1920s and the 1930s it was common to see the name Max Factor credited as responsible for a film's "makeup". He even gave us the term "makeup" as in "to make up ones face". Cosmetics were made popular through film but had been available and to the upper classes via cosmetic industrialists Helena Rubinstein and Elizabeth Arden who had founded their empires in New York in 1910.

Early costume designers for film were often from theatre backgrounds. With continuing improvements in the quality of film and lenses the costume designers' work needed to be sharper and able to stand up to closer scrutiny. During the time of the studio system, now referred to as Hollywood's golden age, there were four costume designers whose work had a significant effect on women's wardrobes—Edith Head, Orry Kelly, Gilbert Adrian and Cecil Beaton. The period between 1930 and 1940 was the pinnacle of women's film and fashion plate films.

Fashion plate film is a term given to films of that period which had a contemporary setting and modern dress—often for these pictures there was a bigger spend on the star's wardrobe than on the rights to the film. Films such as *The Women*, 1939, starring Norma Shearer and Joan Crawford was shot in black and white but included an original ten-minute Technicolor fashion show mid-way through the film. This section acted as a vehicle to introduce the new seasons looks to female audiences. Female filmgoers knew that these films would showcase the coming trends of the season. Within the cinematic fashion show the look of the clothing was never too extreme or too ahead of its time—the designers had to design the costumes eight months before a film's nationwide release and therefore the looks could not be totally current.

Throughout the 1920s film costume was ignored by *Vogue* and other high fashion publications. In the 1930s Hollywood replaced Paris as the oracle of fashion, especially for American women, and *Vogue* began to acknowledge this. The magazine featured some of Hollywood's more aristocratic-looking stars as models. Until the 1950s there were very few professional working models—the women featured in *Vogue* were often society women who were well connected and depicted glamour thought social status.

Previous Page: An example of the popular Butterick's pattern, circa 1950. The company's founder, Ebenezer Butterick, was an American inventor, manufacturer, and fashion business executive who utilised the popularity of cinema in his business.

Left: Cosmetic specialist Max Factor, 1904–1996, examines the quality of Greek singer Kitza Kazaco's makeup, at Lime Grove Studios, London, 1955. Photograph by Terry Fincher/ Keystone/Getty Images.

Joan Crawford, 1934, displays the popular 1930s silhouette.

Opposite Left: Mae West, riding in a carriage, circa 1933.

Opposite Right: Clara Bow was one of the first 'it girls', who rose to fame in the silent film era of the 1920s and was renowned for her 'bow' shaped lips cultivated by Max Factor.

COSTUME DESIGN

The main designers in the golden age of Hollywood made a significant impact on women's fashions from the 1930s until the end of the 1950s, when the star system was coming to an end. Travis Banton, 1898–1958, was the first of these designers. He came to Hollywood in 1924 after having launched a gown shop in New York. Through the shop Banton dressed the Ziegfeld Follies, a series of elaborate theatrical productions on Broadway in New York. Banton came to the attention of the studios after being noticed by Mary Pickford, one part of Hollywood's first power couple. Douglas Fairbank and Mary Pickford founded United Artists with Charlie Chaplin.

It was Travis Banton who designed Pickford's wedding dress and is mostly remembered for the work he did for Mae West in *I'm No Angel*, 1933, and *Belles of the 90s*, 1934. He also designed for Marlene Dietrich, proving costume for some of her most memorable roles in *Shanghai Express*, 1932, *The Scarlet Empress*, 1934, and *The Devil is a Woman*, 1935. It was these roles which inspired the look for the recording artist Madonna in the 1980s. Banton's work is now mostly forgotten and he is most commonly remembered for being the mentor to another costume designer, Edith Head.

During the 1930s Gilbert Adrian, 1903–1959, more commonly
known just as Adrian, was credited as the costume designer on
over 250 films. The majority of these films were for MGM where
he designed most of Greta Garbo's wardrobe, notably for the films
Grand Hotel, 1932, and *Camille*, 1936. He also worked closely with Joan
Crawford on what were regarded as women's fashion films. Adrian
was most famous for his 'above table' design work, creating the box
square shoulders for Crawford which were to be an important and
aspirational part of the 1940s silhouette. Of all the costume designers
of this period, Adrian's work was the most difficult to re-create as
his designs were often made up of numerous panel pieces. One of
his gowns, for the film *Letty Lynton*, 1932, a white dress with huge puff
sleeves and plentiful ruffles, was to create a trend that would last the
entire decade. The fan magazines of the time claimed that 500,000
copies of this dress were made but more recent research by Charlotte
Cornelia Herzog and Jane Marie Gaines, in their book *Stardom: Industry
of Desire*, 1991, cannot support this claim. This does not detract
from the influence of the studios at this time of which Adrian was
a major influence. Adrian left MGM when Greta Garbo completed
her last film, *Two Faced Woman*, 1941, claiming that: "When Garbo left
Hollywood so did the glamour."

ADRIAN

Another of the famous costume designers of the period was Orry Kelly, 1897–1964, born in New South Wales, Australia, where he worked as a window display artist before emigrating to America. Kelly mainly worked for Warner Brothers before moving on to Universal, RKO, Twentieth Century Fox and finally MGM. Kelly was responsible for dressing some of the main film icons of the late 1930s into the 1940s and 50s. He provided costumes for Bette Davis in *Jezebel*, 1938, Ingrid Bergman in *Casablanca*, 1942, Rosalind Russell in *Auntie Mame*, 1958, and the costumes for Marilyn Monroe in *Some Like it Hot*, 1959.

Opposite Top: Greta Garbo, 1912. Garbo was a Swedish-born actress during Hollywood's golden age.

Opposite Bottom: Marlene Dietrich, 1955. Dietrich is considered to be the first German actress to flourish in Hollywood and is an entertainment icon of the twentieth century.

Top: Marylin Monroe in a promotional photograph for the film *The Prince and the Showgirl*, 1957. Monroe is an undisputed cultural icon. She was dressed by Orry Kelly in the cult film *Some Like it Hot*, 1959. Monroe's fame surpassed that of any other entertainer of her time.

EDITH HEAD

Left: Grace Kelly wore this stunning dress for her marriage to Rainier III, Prince of Monaco in 1956. The dress, designed by Edith Head, had a massive impact on the design of wedding dresses for the rest of the decade.

Opposite: American actor, Carroll Baker, wears a costume from the film, *Harlow*, 1965. The costume was designed by Edith Head, who is holding a sketch of her creation. Film producer Joseph E Levine stands on the left. Photograph by Hulton Archive/Getty Images.

No other woman in Hollywood picked up more Academy Awards than Edith Head, 1897–1981, who collected 35 in total—a reflection of her influence and longevity in costume design. Head had originally worked for Paramount as Travis Banton's assistant and it was only with his departure that she became head designer, a position she retained for 44 years.

Head worked well with female stars as was often requested by them personally. Her work as a designer dates from the 1940s on films such as *Double Indemnity*, 1944, where she dressed Barbara Stanwyck and *All About Eve*, 1950, with Bette Davis. Head is mostly remembered for her work with cool blondes in Alfred Hitchcock films, such as Grace Kelly in *Rear Window*, 1954, and *To Catch a Thief*, 1956, and Kim Novak in *Vertigo*, 1958. Predominantly, the films Head was involved with had a contemporary setting and would depict contemporary dress inspired by Paris fashions, showcased in glamorous settings. These films were known as fashion plate films because of their fashion content.

One of Edith Head's creations played its part in a real life fairytale: a wedding dress worn by Grace Kelly, in her marriage to Prince Rainier of Monaco. The dress was the wedding gift from Paramount to the retiring star Kelly. This dress was to have bigger impact on wedding dresses in the 1950s than that worn by Princess Elizabeth in her wedding to Prince Philip, despite the princesses' dress being designed by the royal favourite, Norman Hartnell. To many the dress Head created for Kelly's marriage was the perfect wedding gown, considered fit for a real princess. Hollywood, through film, had been informing the public for almost half a century on the ideal outfit for any occasion. Kelly's dress was Hollywood's version of the perfect wedding gown for a real life royal romance.

Despite her critical acclaim there was one Oscar that some felt Head should have shared with the couturier Hubert de Givenchy. This was the 1958 Oscar for the costumes in *Funny Face*, starring Audrey Hepburn. The premis for this film is of a young book shop assistant that is plucked to be the face of the glamour magazine, *Quality*. The female lead, Hepburn, is then featured wearing the latest Paris couture for the publication. The feel of *Funny Face* is totally in keeping with the period, as the decade was the highpoint in the life of French couture. The film is all the more believable, as Audrey Hepburn's costumes were actual couture garments— the fashion images in the film are even the work of Richard Avedon, one of the greatest fashion photographers of the century. The costumes for *Funny Face* won the Oscar which was collected by Head as she was the studio's head designer. However, the wardrobe for the film had actually been chosen by Hepburn herself from the budding collection of new French designer, Givenchy. It was the costumes worn by Hepburn that had been voted for, not just the remainder designed by Head, and therefore there should have been some acknowledgement to Givenchy alongside the Paramount designer.

Despite the decline of the studio system at the end of the 1950s, the increasing demands from the stars has meant increasing collaborations between the world of high fashion and cinema. This also happened previously under the studio system where surrealist courtier, Shaparelli, had designed for Marlene Detreich and Mae West. Film has always been, and continues to be, able to influence the audience's opinion in terms of what is deemed current. Both on and off screen Hepburn was predominantly dressed by Givenchy in films, although it was not only with his clothing that she changed fashion at street level. *My Fair Lady,* 1964, with costumes by Cecli Beaton caused a change in women's footwear almost overnight. In the film, as well as in the original Beaton-designed stage production, the female characters dressed in pointed shoes with low stiletto heals. This style of shoe was immediately picked up by women and brought about the sudden end of the square toe, block healed shoes which had been prevalent until then.

Many of today's designers are indebted to film and the role that it has played in introducing their work, and more importantly their name, to a wider audience. From Ralph Lauren in the 1970s with his costumes for *The Great Gatsby*, 1974, starring Mia Farrow to *American Gigolo*, 1980, starring Richard Gere in suits by Armani or *The Cook, The Thief, His Wife and Her Lover*, 1989, with costumes by Jean Paul Gaultier. Film has the ability to raise the public's awareness of the designers work. In so doing film can create a desire to own a piece of the glamour of the unattainable cinema icons and their fictional narratives.

Since the 1970s the silver screen has lost some of its influence to the more accessible medium of television. The small box situated in the living rooms of thousands of people has therefore been responsible for creating looks which have had an enormous impact on contemporary culture. From Farrah Fawcett's frosted mane in *Charlie's Angels*, 1976, and the Purdey haircut of the 1970s, to the 1990s and the 'Rachel' haircut from the television sitcom *Friends,* the power of the small screen can not be underestimated—think of the cultural phenomenon that is *Sex and the City* and its legions of fashion followers.

Not every reference on television is positive for designers. This can be seen in the 1990s comedy series *Absolutely Fabulous*. This sharp and witty satire parodied the excess of London's Fashion PR in the late 1980s but it also had a negative effect on how certain brands were perceived by the public—most notably Lacroix. The label, founded by Christian Lacroix, became a byword for the all the excess of fashion yet the couture house had only started in the mid-1980s.

GUINEA DRESS

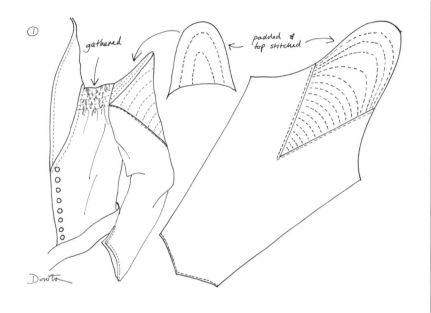

① gathered — padded & top stitched

Dowton

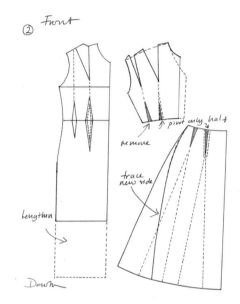

② Front

remove — pivot only half

trace new side

Lengthen

Dowton

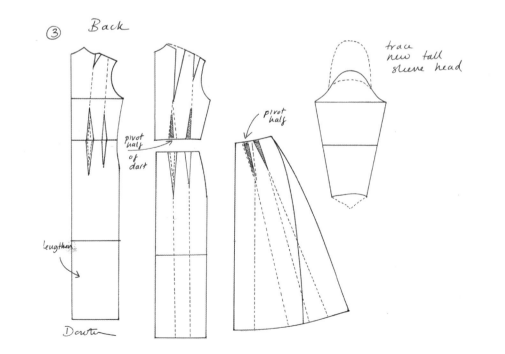

③ Back

pivot half of dart

Lengthen

Dowton

pivot half

trace new tall sleeve head

THIS GUINEA DRESS WAS ORIGINALLY PIONEERED BY JOHN LEWIS. THE WEDDING DRESS HAS A COVER BUTTON FRONT DETAIL AND EXTENDED PADDED SLEEVE, A PADDED ELIZABETHAN-BASED COLLAR AND A PADDED HEM. THE SKIRT OF THE DRESS IS CUT ON THE BIAS TO AVOID THE USE OF THE USUAL HIP DARTS AND PROVIDE A MORE FITTED LOOK. THE PADDING AT THE HEM ENABLES THE DRESS TO HANG REGALLY AND NOT CLING TO THE BODY.

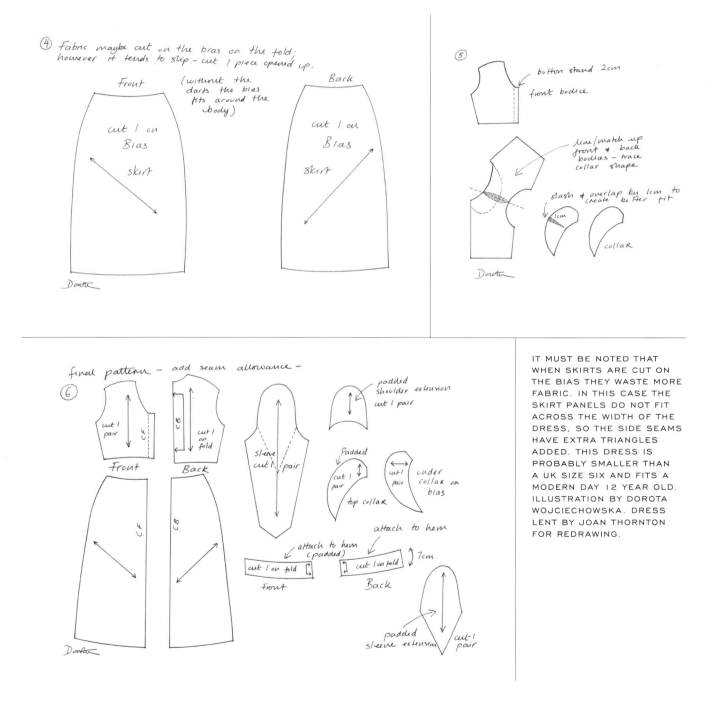

④ Fabric maybe cut on the bias on the fold; however it tends to slip - cut 1 piece opened up.

Front   (without the darts the bias fits around the body)   Back

cut 1 on Bias Skirt

cut 1 on Bias Skirt

Dorota

⑤

button stand 2cm
front bodice

line/match up front & back bodices - trace collar shape

slash & overlap by 1cm to create better fit

1cm

collar

Dorota

final pattern - add seam allowance -

⑥

cut 1 pair   CF

CB   cut 1 on fold

Front   Back

CF

CB

Dorota

padded shoulder extension cut 1 pair

sleeve cut 1 pair

Padded cut 1 pair

top collar

cut 1 pair   under collar on bias

attach to hem

attach to hem (padded)

cut 1 on fold   cut 1 on fold   7cm

Front   Back

padded sleeve extension   cut 1 pair

IT MUST BE NOTED THAT WHEN SKIRTS ARE CUT ON THE BIAS THEY WASTE MORE FABRIC. IN THIS CASE THE SKIRT PANELS DO NOT FIT ACROSS THE WIDTH OF THE DRESS, SO THE SIDE SEAMS HAVE EXTRA TRIANGLES ADDED. THIS DRESS IS PROBABLY SMALLER THAN A UK SIZE SIX AND FITS A MODERN DAY 12 YEAR OLD. ILLUSTRATION BY DOROTA WOJCIECHOWSKA. DRESS LENT BY JOAN THORNTON FOR REDRAWING.

1940–1950

*

FASHION AND CONFLICT CC41

As a reaction to the Second World War the public began recycling of 1930s knitwear to create garments as if from new in the 1940s. The politically enforced make-do-and-mend austerity of the Second World War was the prevailing trend of the period as garments were remade and no excess fabric was used. Explored here is the use of unconventional fabrics, traditionally reserved for the other industries, to create fashions of the day, for example parachute material utilised in wedding dresses.

WAR AND FASHION

Fashion and war are not two things that would people would normally combine. People naturally assume fashion is something which can only happen in a stable society, whose members have a great deal of leisure time in order to pursue their personal desires. However, in times of war and conflict, despite the social upheaval, fashion does not disappear. The look of the day may not be Parisian couture but the clothing that is produced is nonetheless a semiotic expression of the time. Conflict has inspired the collections of several designers such as Hussein Chalayan whose coffee table skirt, 2000, was inspired by the 1974 conflict in Cyprus. This division of the country between Turkey and Greece meant many had to leave their homes and take with them only what they could carry. Therefore

Chalayan's design sees the multifunction aspect of fashion as coffee table becomes a skirt.

In the semiotics of fashion there is a political message contained within any particular look which can be understood by those who know the reference points. The muted blue colour scheme of eighteenth century Whig parties used a colouring that was banned from the royal court as it was the opposing colour to the ruling government of George III. Fashion can be seen as coded messages which speak of where society is positioned at a particular point in time and reflecting the social and economic culture.

Previous Page: A woman reapplies her makeup between air raids, a common sight in the 1940s.

Left: The Nagasaki nuclear bomb explosion, as seen from the air, August 1945.

Right: Pearl Bailey, 1918–1990, was an American singer and actress. After appearing in vaudeville she made her Broadway debut in *Saint Louis Woman,* 1946. Photograph Carl Van Vechten.

The Second World War changed life for the civilian population unlike any other war that had previously taken place. It did not just take place on battlefields but effected the whole population of Europe from 1939 to 1945. This was felt by the civilian public through the long reaching missiles, the close-proximity aircraft bombers positioned directly over civilian homes and the embargo set up by Germany to stop any aid and relief reaching Britain during the period. This calculated, systematic closing down of Europe allowed other areas of the world to take a lead in fashion and to look to their own designers and markets with renewed interest. The majority of couture fashion houses in Paris had closed in 1940 with the German occupation of the country. Even if the couture houses had stayed open, many of their high class clientele were involved in war work and therefore not leading the lives that suited couture. Although America did not enter the War until 1941, its inhabitants would not cross the Atlantic due to the danger involved. Americans turned to their own dressmakers for their fashion needs and this is one of the main reasons that American designers on New York's Fifth Avenue, such as Norman Norell, became the creators of the look for American women. It could even be argued that the Second World War gave the American fashion system a chance to flourish and find its own aesthetic without the influence of couture Paris.

CC41

  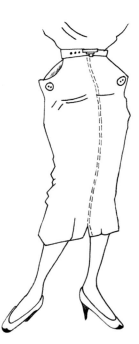

Due to the War there was a shift in the entire manufacturing industry as factories and their workforces were redeployed to make munitions and uniforms for the war effort. In recognition of this fact the government introduced the CC41 label in 1941. The, now famous, logo, which looks like two round cheeses with a small wedge taken out of each, was designed by Reginald Shipp, the two Cs standing for Clothing Control. It was not that the government wanted to restrict the public's consumption as a whole; CC41 attempted to make sure that what was available was fairly distributed amongst the people. CC41, launched in 1941, was the clothing version of the rationing that had been introduced on food in 1940. From 1941 clothing could only be purchased with coupons and additional money. Initially, there was an annual allowance of 66 coupons per person.

A short jacket or a wool dress would cost seven coupons so the public were advised to use them sparingly. As the war continued the number of coupons was reduced to 48 and eventually to 36 coupons in 1945 as the struggle became even harder and Britain was forced be almost totally self-supporting.

Clothing which was worthy of the CC41 label had to be well made and have no frills, or even buttons, than was strictly necessary. The government introduced sumptuary laws which regulated how long a skirt could be and the total yardage of material allowed for a garment. These items would be sold in stores such as Marks and Spencer but were cheaper than any clothing which did not bear the label.

Previous Page: Woman aircraft worker, Vega Aircraft Corporation, Burbank, California, checking electrical assemblies, 1942. Photography David Bransby.

Opposite: The Birth of a Gown, a creation by British photographer and fashion designer Cecil Beaton for German actress Lilli Palmer in her film *Beware of Pity,* 1946. Photograph by Popperfoto, April 1945.

Top Left and Centre: Both images depict a close up of a 1940s CC41 housecoat from Marks and Spencer. Each is dressed with a diamanté clip as it would have been styled for other functions in the 1940s.

Top Right: The slim and cropped CC41 waist. Illustration by Charlotte Craig, 2008.

Due to the lack of clothing and new fabrics to make fashion garments, magazines promoted the recycling of garments or reworking of other fabric items to create clothing. Noted examples are a pillow case made into summer shorts or, more famously, the use of unusual fabrics to make wedding dresses—either parachute fabric or blackout material which had been bleached. Bridal gowns of the period were often shared between many brides as they could not access either suitable material or enough of a quantity to make a gown.

The overall female silhouette changed during the Second World War and became vertically exaggerated as women adopted platform shoes and piled their hair high. This caused a lengthening of the silhouette which was further emphasised due to the narrowness of the skirts and the predominantly box shapes of jackets. With the restrictions on clothing there was a greater demand by women for headwear which was often home-produced and served a number of roles—hiding unkempt hair away from view and keeping hair well away from the machinery in the factories. Headwear such as turbans and other novel ideas were worn by women to keep up their moral virtue and retain a certain amount of femininity when fashion allowed little or no room for embellishment.

Newspapers and women's magazines of the period supported the war effort by featuring articles which promoted a make-do-and-mend ethos to the British public. *Mrs Sew and Sew*, amongst others, promoted the idea of recycling clothing and would give tips to ensure that all available fabric was used to its full potential. It is mainly due to this reason that there is almost no 1930s knitwear available in the current vintage market. These garments would have been undone in order to use the yarn to make the 1940s garments which were required at the time.

Right: 1940s Christian Dior cocktail dress. Image courtesy Aaron Walker, 2008.

Opposite: The silhouette of the Second World War, 1943. London's austerity fashions, which became popular during the war. Fashion design by Worth.

American glamour model and pin-up girl Bettie Page displays the reintroduction of sexuality through dress, 1955. Photograph by *Archive Photos*.

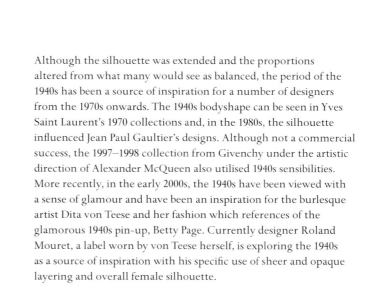

Although the silhouette was extended and the proportions altered from what many would see as balanced, the period of the 1940s has been a source of inspiration for a number of designers from the 1970s onwards. The 1940s bodyshape can be seen in Yves Saint Laurent's 1970 collections and, in the 1980s, the silhouette influenced Jean Paul Gaultier's designs. Although not a commercial success, the 1997–1998 collection from Givenchy under the artistic direction of Alexander McQueen also utilised 1940s sensibilities. More recently, in the early 2000s, the 1940s have been viewed with a sense of glamour and have been an inspiration for the burlesque artist Dita von Teese and her fashion which references of the glamorous 1940s pin-up, Betty Page. Currently designer Roland Mouret, a label worn by von Teese herself, is exploring the 1940s as a source of inspiration with his specific use of sheer and opaque layering and overall female silhouette.

Rationing did not recede in Britain in 1945 with the end of the War. The country needed to address the devastation the War had had on the population and country and rationing was a way of gradually returning to normality. In Britain the government kept issuing ration books until 1949 and the ultimate demise of rationing did not take place until 1952. When the War ended the public wanted to return to some form of equilibrium; not just to exist but to actually enjoy life again. This feeling of wanting to return to some semblance of what life had been like coincided with the Theatre of Fashion exhibition.

Following the liberation of Paris in 1946 the couture houses re-opened. After the long period of inactivity there was a travelling exhibition, Theatre of Fashion—a collection of miniature models dressed by the many fashion houses of Paris. This exhibition served to promote the new Parisian fashion ideas and generate interest in the city's design houses. The Theatre of Fashion exhibition that directly followed the War had garments made on quarter scale mannequins as material was still in short supply. This way of working was not unique at the time as many students, learning their craft in fashion, would work at this scale in order to solve problems without wasting vast amounts of fabric.

TWEED SUIT

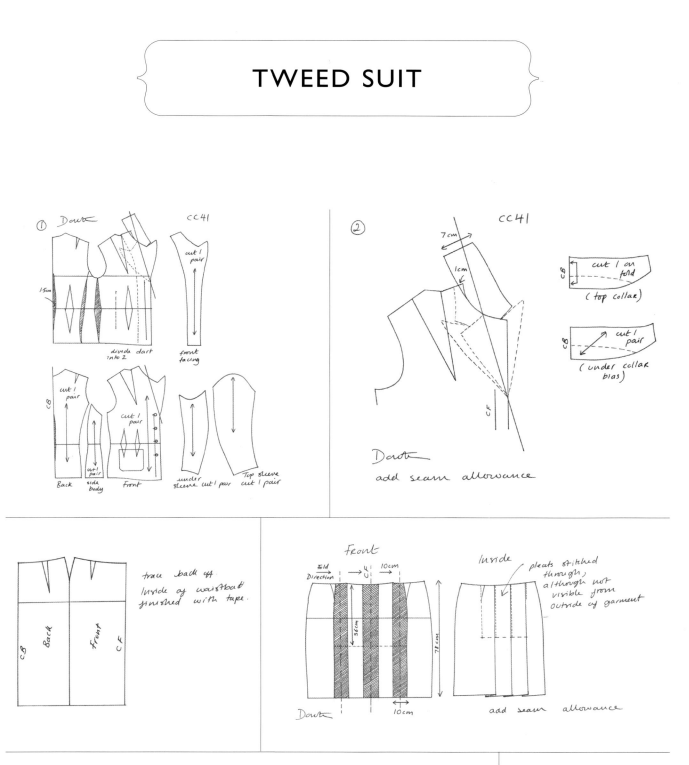

THESE PATTERN PIECES DERIVED FROM THE ACTUAL SUIT. HEAVY TWEED SUIT WITH DETAIL OF TAILORED BUTTON HOLE AND SIDE OPENING. DUE TO EXPENSE AND SCARCITY OF TRIMS DURING THE WAR, PRESS-STUDS OF VARYING SIZES WERE USED. ILLUSTRATION BY DOROTA WOJCIECHOWSKA. GARMENT COURTESY JOAN THORNTON.

Opposite: This woman wears a fitted tweed suit, similar in style to the pattern pieces above. Here the suit is accessorised with a pill box hat and red basket handbag. Photograph by *Housewife* magazine, January 1955.

1950–1960

*

THE BATTLE OF THE TWO GIANT COLOSSI

There was a rebirth of fashion after the strict fabric rationing during the Second World War. As nations recovered from times of hardship, fashion as a means of expressing release from standardised, functional workwear was enjoyed. The luscious fashion houses of 1950s Paris were re-opened and the diffusion line in fashion became popular in this period. For the first time the youth of society was embraced as being totally current, rather than completely derived from parental control. The flourish in the youth market is undeniable in the 1950s and their influence is still felt today. Women's shape changed during the decade and the unattainable, sexually-charged style of the starlet was revered. Mimicking this ideal 1950s figure required specific undergarments for women.

The 1950s began with strict food and fabric rationing but ended with prosperity and celebration. The Americans and the Soviets entered the space race, literally reaching for the stars after the War years. The influence of the prospect of longevity in space travel was felt in all areas of culture and fashion.

Britain, in the early part of the decade, tried to inject some confidence into a population who had survived the Second World War. In 1951 the Festival of Britain opened at the South Bank Centre, London, in an attempt to represent a land fit for heroes. Britain in the 1950s also entered its second Elizabethan era and the coronation, 1953, saw the television set welcomed into many homes as the population clamoured to see this historic event televised for the first time.

During the 1950s Hollywood narrativea and celebrity endorsement, suggested the aspiration of every career girl was to land herself a man and settle down to a life of domestic bliss and homemaking. This notion is seen as a constant norm in the films of Doris Day. Also promoting the idea of the height of female achievement being ultra-femininity were the newly emerging celebrity chefs Elizabeth David and Fanny Craddock. Meals were no longer quickly prepared between shifts in the factory. Women were now introduced to *cordon bleu* cookery and situated back in the home.

After the austerity of the War years, women wanted to once again connect with their fashion-expressed femininity which had been somewhat subdued by rationing during the War years. In the days of less restrictive rationing indulgence in meterage was once again enjoyed. Key focal points in the overall silhouette included the exaggeration of the relationship between the waist and bust—sensuality was once again on the agenda.

Previous Page: Dior model Jean Dawnay (Princess George Galitzine), 1956, posing with champagne and furs in this editorial shoot. Photograph by Hulton Archive/Getty Images.

The Oscar-nominated American actress, Ava Gardner, strikes a provocative pose in this leopard print 1950s attire, circa 1953.

SOPHIA LOREN

Key fashion protagonists of 1950s included Christian Dior, Cristóbal Balenciaga, Pierre Balmain, Louis Feraud and Hubert de Givenchy. These designers devised a new aesthetic which would run for many years and be copied and referenced by many modern day designers.

Hollywood recognised the optimistic mood of the 1950s, offering the image of glamorous, voluptuous and confident women who were very much in tune with the fashion *zeitgeist*. Film stars were inspiration to many women both in both America and Britain. In cinema the iconic films of the decade explored the changing post-war social landscape and a greater element of realism was represented on cinema screens. Influential films of the period included: *The African Queen*, 1951, *Singing in the Rain*, 1952, *From Here to Eternity*, 1953, *Gentleman Prefer Blondes*, 1953, *Roman Holiday*, 1953, *On the Waterfront*, 1954, *Rebel Without a Cause*, 1955, *Rock Around the Clock*, 1956, *Baby Doll*, 1956, *Vertigo*, 1958, *Some Like it Hot*, 1959, *Ben Hur*, 1959, and *North by Northwest*, 1959.

Sophia Loren was born in 1934 in Rome, Italy. Also known as Sofia Lazzaro and Sofia Scicolene her life began in poverty. Loren was bought up by her mother, a piano teacher who was also an aspiring actress who had been left by the father of her children. The young Loren lived with her grandmother and sister, waiting tables until she entered a beauty contest at 14, giving her a taste for glamour and a genuine avenue for seeking a new life. After a hand-to-mouth existence she enrolled in acting classes and was selected as an extra in the film *Quo Vadis*, 1951, which launched her international career. Loren was soon cast as a leading lady, delighting audiences with her sultry looks. Some of her films include: *Boy on a Dolphin*, 1957, *The Pride and the Passion*, 1957, *Desire Under the Elms*, 1958, *The Fall of the Roman Empire*, 1964, *The Millionairess*, 1960, *Arabesque*, 1966, *El Cid*, 1961, and latterly *Grumpier Old Men*, 1995. In the 1960s Loren was one of the world's most popular actresses.

The cultural and sexual icon Sophia Loren, 1955. Loren became one of the most recognisable faces of the 1950s. Photograph by *Silver Screen*.

THE
TEENAGER

The 1950s saw the birth of what is now known as the teenager in America, a phenomenon that crossed the Atlantic as prosperity returned to Europe. Before the 1950s society's youth were mirror images of their parents until they entered the world of work (where uniforms would define their look). Youth cults such as the teddy boy were to be the first recognisable subculture with their drapes (a long knee length, single breasted wool jacket with narrow contrasting lapels and cuffs either of velvet or satin and plenty of pockets), reminiscent of Edwardian men's suits, the term teddy is an abbreviation of the name Edward. With the growing youth market there was also new icons who came notably from the new music genre of rock'n'roll and the influence of American artists such as Elvis Presley had global appeal. Many in Europe found the American influence worrying and feared a dumbing down of culture in general.

Elvis Presely promoting the film *Jailhouse Rock*, 1957. Elvis was seen as the living embodiment of the cult of the teenager.

MY AIM IS TO SAVE
WOMEN FROM NATURE

CHRISTIAN DIOR

DIOR'S NEW LOOK

In the 1950s the new French fashion designer of the day was
Christian Dior, 1905–1957, who, with the financial backing of
Marcel Buossac, had given the world his New Look in 1947. Dior
began his career selling fashion sketches but in 1938 he joined
Robert Pignet, moving to Lelong in 1942 where he worked
alongside the fashion designer, Pierre Balmain. Boussac offered
Dior the opportunity to open his own couture house and the
first collection was called Corolle, because of its huge skirts which
spread like corollas from fitted bodies with tiny waists. Although
the collection was officially named Corolle, Carmel Snow, the
editor of American style magazine, *Harpers Bazaar*, commented at
the time: "Christian, we love your new look." New Look has been
the officially understood title of the collection ever since. The
designs featured narrow shoulders, calf length full skirts and
padded hips; a complete contrast to the padded shoulders and
straight skirts of the Second World War. Femininity was now
on full display and not frugal. Despite the New Look being
launched in the 1940s it was in the 1950s that admiration
and universal success called for Dior. Later in the decade
a more slimline pencil silhouette was added to his range.

Previous Page: This evening dress was
designed by Yves Saint Laurent for
Dior, Cirque d'Hiver, Paris, 1955. The
dress is from one of the most famous
fashion photographs of all time:
Dovima with the Elephants by world
renowned fashion photographer
Richard Avedon.

Opposite: Model, 1948, wearing formal
navy cocktail dress by Christian Dior,
featuring short skirt with a large bow,
scissor panel in satin with a camisole
top. Photograph by Nina Leen.
Courtesy of Time Life Pictures.

BALENCIAGA

A key signature of Cristóbal Balenciaga's design was the cantilever cut which produced a slimmer silhouette on a curvier form. Being Spanish, Balenciaga's love for the native dance, the flamenco, inspired this look. His dresses rose at the front and trailed to the back, allowing air to enter which, with the wearer's motion, billowed out behind creating a somewhat regal appearance. These dresses, executed in silk gazar (a loosely woven silk with a crisp finish), became linked with cocktail dresses. Sleeve lengths and proportions were played with and sleeveless dresses were designed, both being accessorised with gloves. *Decollete*, or low-necked pieces were becoming more common with a discreet length and a much more formal train at the back.

Both Dior and Balenciaga were subtle rivals in their design aesthetic. Each fashion house's silhouettes exaggerated femininity but it can be argued that Dior's garments appeared to be more wearable as the female form did not have such exaggerated curves. Balenciaga's gowns, on the other hand, were more conceptual and sculptural. Dior's shapes were a throwback to an earlier era, remimisent of a golden age, and the overall silhouette was derived from the Edwardian period. The period's emphasis of female curves and the sheer mass of fabric made the garments unsuitable for women in the workplace. Balenciaga's garments were more challenging and avant garde, creating powerful visuals. It was therefore powerful women who were required to wear and endorse them; the fashion photographs created by Irving Penn for contemporary fashion magazine *Bazaar* for example.

Three women model evening dresses by Cristóbal Balenciaga, inspired by Henri de Toulouse Lautrec paintings, New York, 1951. Balenciaga introduced couture shapes to the world and was referred to as "the master of us all" by contemporary Christian Dior. Balenciaga's bubble skirts and feminine, ultra-modern shapes were trademarks of the house. Photograph by Gjon Mili of Time Life Pictures.

IN BALENCIAGA YOU WERE THE ONLY WOMAN IN THE ROOM—NO OTHER WOMAN EXISTED

DIANA VREELAND

An impression of the 1940s
silhouette. Illustration by Charlotte
Craig, 2008.

PIERRE BALMAIN

The famous designer, Pierre Balmain, was born in 1914 in Paris, France. As an elegant and sophisticated creator of garments Balmain said that, "dressmaking is the architecture of movement". Balmain's father was the owner of a wholesale drapery business and is seen by many as the catalyst for Balmain's first interest in fabric manipulation. Having studied at Ecole des beaux-arts, France, Balmain went to work for British fashion designer, Edward Molyneux. Balmain joined Lucien Lelong after the Second World War, opening his own fashion house in 1945.

As a designer Balmain became intrinsically linked to glamour and film stars. He was nominated for the Tony Award for his costume design and won the Drama Desk Award for Outstanding Costume Design for the film *Happy New Year*, 1980. Broadway theatre credits for Balmain include the costumes for Katharine Hepburn in *The Millionairess*, 1952, and Josephine Baker for her eponymous 1964 revue. Balmain also was a costume designer for 16 films, including the Brigitte Bardot showcase *And God Created Woman*, 1956, and designed on-screen wardrobes for the actresses Vivien Leigh and Mae West as well as Ava Gardner.

Pierre Balmain and Ruth Ford,
photographed by Carl Van Vechten,
November 1947.

GIVENCHY

The Givenchy design house was founded in 1952 by designer Hubert de Givenchy and is mainly remembered for being instrumental in the public persona of Audrey Hepburn who, throughout the late 1950s and early 1960s, was one of Hollywood's highest earning stars. Givenchy stepped down from his position as premier fashion designer in 1995. John Galliano succeeded him as designer for the fashion house and was later replaced by Alexander McQueen. In 2001, designer Julien McDonald was appointed as artistic director for Givenchy's women's lines, while in 2003 Ozwald Boateng was appointed the head designer for the men's range. Givenchy clothing lines include haute couture as well as ready-to-wear fashions. The Givenchy legacy has had longevity well into the current decade.

High-buttoned cuffs with black, embroidered ruffles falling over them are one of many Hubert de Givenchy treatments of the big sleeve, an important and iconic fashion trend in the 1950s. Photograph by Nat Farbman. Image courtesy Time Life Pictures, circa 1956.

In order to re-create the 1950s film star glamour and silhouette, dresses needed to be worn with the appropriate undergarments, otherwise the accentuated female curves could not be naturally achieved. 1950s waists were nipped and breasts uplifted and numerous undergarments were worn such girdles, bras, corselets and controlettes to obtain these shapes. Garments were reinforced with boning set in channels. Traditionally whalebone had been used, then steel and latterly plastic, which offered more flexibility for the wearer. Incredibly sturdy girdles were available, although more women opted for the roll-ons and bras. Twilfit was one of the main 1950s household underwear brands. All-in-ones were very much favoured—the corselet by John Roussel was in great demand during 1953, having been featured in *Queen* magazine. The corselet's particular appeal was due its particular cleavage gap which allowed for a low cut *décolletage*. Another item featured in *Queen* was the marquise, which was strapless corselet with a deep plunge.

UNDERGARMENTS

In the 1950s bras were being produced in washable, more flexible, fabrics, such as nylon trimmed with *broderie anglaise* and lace. Many women made their own underwear using a wide range of textiles from parachute nylon, parachute silk and old wedding dresses in the period. By the 1970s suspender belts were disappearing due to the invention of pantyhose and stay-up stockings, although their sexy feminine appeal has remained to this very day.

The conical bra was also referred to as a sweater glamour bra, where the wearer emulated stars such as Jane Russell and Lana Turner. The breast cups were literally conically shaped and stitched for further re-enforcement. The female form was both exaggerated and celebrated through this accentuation. The conical bra was a hidden garment at the time but became a feature of Madonna's costume for her *Blonde Ambition* tour, 1990, designed for her by Jean-Paul Gaultier. Together Madonna and Gaultier challenged preconceptions of undergarments as overgarments, keeping their appeal sexy despite exaggerating the form. Other examples of undergarments brought into the public domain and styled on the 1950s include the clothing adopted by erotic performer Dita von Teese. Part of her extensive repertoire not only includes vintage dresses but a vast medley of vintage female underwear.

The structured undergarments were in many instances constricting, but they did make a big comeback in the 1980s with the power dressing and ultra strong female persona. Television fuelled this rebirth with programmes such as *Dynasty*, 1981–1989, where Joan Collins lounged in all-in-one teddies and bodysuits. The 1980s interpretation on the corsets and corselets was more forgiving, having been produced in more flexible fabrics by manufacturers such as Wolford.

Opposite: The 1950s bodyshape was achieved with help from underwear like the controlette depicted in this advert. Image circa 1955.

Top: Oscar winning American film actress Gloria Grahame displays the conical bra in all its glory, circa 1954.

MARKS AND SPENCER

By the 1950s Marks and Spencer was establishing itself as the best chain store offering ready-to-wear garments. Their clothes were not the cheapest at the time, but were the best value for money because of their longevity. During this time they started to emulate Parisian glamour at more affordable prices and consequently introduced fashion to a wider market.

The trend of interpreting and of offering the consumer the dream of the designer-inspired garments was delivered by other high street outlets such as Wallis, which gained a reputation for producing Chanel copies at a more affordable prices in the late 1950s and into the 1960s. This trend continues to this very day, with the high street shop or chain, notably the Spanish store Zara, mimicking the catwalk collections. For this reason glamour and the ability to remain stylish is available to every woman at an affordable price.

The tiny waist and wide skirt of the 1950s silhouette. Illustration by Charlotte Craig, 2008.

Opposite: Marks and Spencer skirts from the 1950s. By 1950, all Marks and Spencer goods were sold under the Saint Michael label. The company put its main emphasis on quality, but for most of its history had a reputation for offering value for money to the customer.

1960–1970

*

BUBBLING UP! YOUTH REVOLUTION AND COUNTERCULTURE

The London fashion scene really took hold in the 1960s and greatly influenced youth culture all over the world. Popstars, rock stars and other musicians embraced the newfound rebellious culture of the teenager during this period and their feminised fashion decisions became expressive streetwear for legions of adoring fans. Bands like The Beatles, the Rolling Stones and artists such as Jimi Hendrix reshaped fashion with their unisexual, androgynous looks and legions of screaming female admirers followed their fashions. The introduction of retro in fashion is explored here, through the key referencing of contemporary film and print and the counterculture which ran alongside the mass appeal.

1960s

To fully understand the mindset of young people in the 1960s, it is important to understand the social and political landscape. The 1960s and 70s was an incredibly formative era, both socially and economically, which afforded its participants full sensory and creative independence from their parents. The culture of the teenager from the 1950s was a whole new phenomenon at the time whereas, in the 1960s and 70s, youth culture was more explosive and nonconformist in Britain and America. Focusing on the physical impact of fashion, visionaries were creating new silhouettes and introducing new, forward thinking graphic concepts. Music was creating its own genre which evoked a certain mood and shaped a particular sense of being for youth consumers. Ever since the introduction of rock as a sound for the new generation, it has been inseparable from the sociology of youth.

During the 1960s there was double tragedy in the Kennedy household when John F Kennedy was assassinated in November 1963 and his brother Robert Kennedy was assassinated in the presidential candidate election, 1968. During Lyndon Johnson's presidential term (which began in 1964) the civil rights movement came to the fore, inspiring the John Waters' film *Hairspray*, 1988, starring drag persona Divine. President Nixon ended the Vietnam War in 1968, although the period of drafting of troops was extended, and many young men sought to evade it by ripping up their draft papers and crossing the boarder to Canada.

In Britain the Conservative Prime Minister, Harold Macmillan, came into power with the slogan "never had it so good" and the country was introduced for the first time to building schemes, motorways and council housing. Later in the decade the relationship between Christine Keeler, a former model, and the British Minster, John Profumo, became the centre of a scandal as Keeler was also conducting an affair with a the Soviet naval attache, Yevgeny Ivanov. To many this went even further to highlight the changing social landscape in British society and the distrust between the Capitalist West and the Soviet Block grew. Into the latter part of the decade Britain suffered from decay and industrial decline as union power began to grow and there were a series of strikes throughout the country.

During the 1960s, Carnaby Street in Soho, London, became world famous as a hotspot of 'swinging London'. It was a key place for Britain's youth revolutionaries and had a long-term influence on London's shopping, fashion and tourist industries. By the end of the 1960s, Carnaby Street was London's second most visited tourist attraction after Buckingham Palace.

Previous Page: One of the numerous miniskirted models of the 1960s. The miniskirt defined the look of the decade.

Opposite: Jimi Hendrix, 1942–1970, is considered one of the greatest and most influential guitarists in rock music history. After initial success in Europe, he achieved fame in America following his 1967 performance at the Monterey Pop Festival and went on to headline at the iconic Woodstock Festival, 1969.

Top: An American soldier in Vietnam, circa 1962.

The 1945 and post-war generation of teenagers produced the first Western youth subculture—teds, mods, rockers, hippies and punks. Each successive generation has produced its own particular youth subculture which was represented through its taste in clothing and music. Alongside the personal identification with the music came the sense of belonging to a group and the fashion uniform associated with it.

Influential musicians and consequent style makers of the 1960s and 70s include: the Rolling Stones, The Beatles, Jimi Hendrix, The Doors, Frank Zappa and Jefferson Airplane. Their flamboyant stage costumes influenced both fashion designers and society itself. The male protagonists of these bands were dressed in more feminine styles which were adopted by both sexes in the public realm. Their influence appears to be as attractive now as it was in previous decades. Once a style is repeated years after it was initially conceived, it is referred to as 'retro' because of its retrospective nature.

As an aside from the civil rights movement, women were becoming more empowered and liberated with the introduction of the contraceptive pill and experimentation with social modes of behaviour was stimulated by the use of drugs. Particularly associated with this decade are the drugs cannabis and LSD, both of which are simultaneously linked with progression in social culture and the hippy movement.

Civil rights demonstration, circa 1960. The process of moving toward equality under the law was long and tenuous in many countries and protests of this nature were, unfortunately, commonplace.

Quant
1964

BOUTIQUE

The fashion boutique became a new phenomena on the high street, selling designer-led youth fashions rather than practical basics. One of the most famous boutique owners was Mary Quant with her shop Bazaar and Barbara Hulanicki's Magpies' Nest which morphed into Biba later in the decade. The infamous Granny Takes a Trip, the boutique on King's Road, London, was also popular.

The very early 1960s fashions were more conformist, clinging onto the 1950s ideals and style. As the decade continued there was much more experimentation with elements of culture. Fashion started moving away from the 1950s ideal when the miniskirt and minidress hit the streets. The highly revealing and unparalleled mini shocked society. The garment first started appearing in 1965 with British designers like Ossie Clark, Bill Gibb and Mary Quant. Paris too offered their version of the mini with designers such as Yves Saint Laurent, André Courrèges and Emanuel Ungaro. Along side the mini was the short A line shape, echoing reinvention of the trapeze shape from previous decades.

Throughout the decade fabric and graphics were being redefined, with block colours, surreal psychedelic pattern and Pop art graphics. Other advances included the incorporation of nylon into fabric—creating polyester, crimplene and PVC—which changed the hang of clothes and their subsequent care. Wearers were liberated in clothes which suited their lifestyle, music and personality. Teenagers no longer looked like miniature versions of their parents.

France had its own young designers, like Emmanuelle Khanh and Sonia Rykiel, producing ready-to-wear clothing. In America, Betsey Johnson ran the hip New York boutique Paraphernalia and the inventive designer, Rudi Gernreich, introduced the American west coast to vinyl clothing and the monokini, a topless bathing suit.

Opposite: Graphic 1960s patterned minidress and coat by Mary Quant, 1964. Quant is famed for her work on Pop art in fashion and influenced the wardrobes of thousands of women during the decade.

Right: Depiction of the Mary Quant minidress. Illustration by Rosie McGuinness, 2008.

MODS

A key movement of the 1960s was the modernist movement
or mod. The term was originally used in the 1950s to describe
jazz fans. Colin MacInnes' novel *Absolute Beginners*, 1959, describes
a modernist as a young jazz fan who dresses in sharp Italian clothes.
The mods of the 1960s dressed in different attire but the smart,
well-turned-out sensibility was the same. Mod, the cultural genre
as we know it, peaked in the mid-1960s and protagonists were very
distinctive in their style-conscious look. A clean, tailor-made look
with short hair and trademark Parka and Vespa, identified them as
members of this group.

Opposite: Two mod girls in a nightclub
display the female version of the mod
styles with block colours and paired-
down Pop art-inspired graphic shapes,
circa 1965.

Right: The mods wore extremely
tailored clothing. Illustration by Rosie
McGuinness, 2008.

ROCKERS

The rockers were a predominantly male orientated movement, which did not agree with the peaceful attitudes of the hippies. Rockers challenged their morality and upbringing by belonging to a morally dubious chapter and drinking and smoking heavily. Drugs, alcohol and promiscuity were encouraged throughout rocker culture. Long hair, tattoos, big boots and a generally unkempt look was the rocker signature. Women wore female versions of the male ensemble, polished off with brassy makeup. Women were generally treated as possessions and did not have much of their own voice— somewhat of a paradox with what was going on throughout 1960s society. This bad girl image was later adopted by Hollywood with the film *Easy Rider*, 1969, and female rock bands adopted the look, allowing them to compete with their male counterparts. Designers too, for example Versace, used this influence in later decades.

This anti-establishment movement and look lent itself to the counterculture S&M. Role reversal here was quite commonplace with the dominatrix being, essentially, the biker's mole or an actualised rock chick. This look was embraced by designers and is now commonplace on the high street, where schoolgirls can readily transform themselves without really understanding the heritage and connotations.

A modern high end version of the rocker fashion with leather jacket and bag and ubiquitous dark glasses. Illustration by Rosie McGuinness, 2008.

Opposite Left: The typical short sleeved 1960s jacket and minidress from the 1960s. Illustration Charlotte Craig, 2008.

Opposite Right: Pucci print from the late 1970s. This print is in marked contrast to the psychedelic prints which the designer was renowned for in the 1960s. The use of strong colour and the bold pattern still make the garments instantly recognisable as Pucci.

An important 1960s Californian contribution came from the hippy movement, which introduced an alternative lifestyle and politics to contemporary society. The hippy movement had started in the Haight Ashbury region of San Francisco, and came to symbolise the American west coast's liberal politics and a rejection of the Eisenhower-era politics. The hippy look was synonymous with colourful antique and ethnic-inspired clothing. The look was to mix and match items from different eras and cultures, offering an eclectic personal touch. Devotees of the style wore their hair long, went barefoot or wore sandals. Hippies accessorised their outfits with beads, bangles and sometimes painted their faces and bodies.

With the political turmoil in America the hippy movement was very closely associated with the anti-war movement as well as the freedom it afforded through sexual experimentation and drugs. The famous Woodstock festival was the musical climax of this movement and is seen to epitomise the 1960s sensibilities.

With television sets becoming more available and the use of cinema as a powerful informational tool, visual imagery and symbolism were prevalent in the 1960s. Women were being seen as more powerful members of society who were both aware and in control of their own sexuality. The embodiment of this notion is apparent with Diana Rigg in the iconic television show, *The Avengers*, 1961–1969. Dressed in figure-hugging black leather catsuits, Rigg's female self-assurance was visually personified.

With television being introduced into households the actresses, singers and personalities of the time were subliminally influencing audiences on key looks and trends. Not only was this a fashion information tool, but also a powerful visual commentary on social and political issues directly experienced in the home.

America, despite the presidential assassinations, was still an optimistic nation and technological advances in space travel were forging ahead. The space race between Russia and America was in full swing, awakening society's interest and sense of adventure and optimism. Film and television adopted this new scientific genre with open hands. This optimism is again being drawn on for inspiration the 2000s, where metallics are a staple of many collections. The 1960s advances in fabric technology fuelled design experimentation in relation to concept, cut and colour.

RICHARD SHOPS DRESS

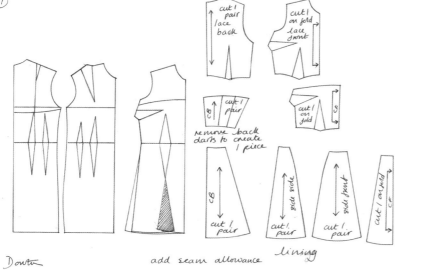

①

cut 1
pair
lace
back

cut 1
on fold
lace
front

cut 1
pair

CB

remove back
darts to create
1 piece

cut 1
on fold

CB

cut 1 on fold
CF

CB

cut 1
pair

side side

cut 1
pair

side front

cut 1
pair

cut 1 on fold
CF

Dorota

add seam allowance

lining

THIS DRESS IS MADE OF BLACK COTTON AND NYLON LACE. THERE IS PLEATED COTTON OVER SKIRT ABOVE THE LINING. THE BODICE IS CONSTRUCTED FROM COTTON OVERLAID WITH LACE AND THE NECK AND ARMHOLES ARE BOUND IN BLACK FABRIC. THIS LOOK IS INSPIRED BY COUTURE GARMENTS SUCH AS THOSE OF BELLVILLE SASSOON. ILLUSTRATION BY DOROTA WOJCIECHOWSKA. DRESS BORROWED FROM SUZI POTTS FOR REDRAWING.

Opposite: Bellville Sassoon 1960s dress. This dress may have been the inspiration for the Richard Shops high street dress of the same era.

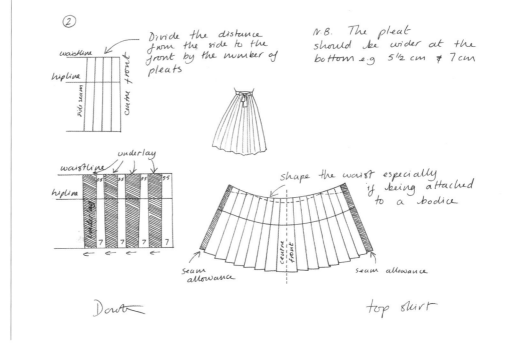

②

waistline

hipline

side seam

centre front

Divide the distance from the side to the front by the number of pleats

N.B. The pleat should be wider at the bottom e.g 5½ cm ÷ 7cm

waistline

underlay

hipline

55   55   55   55

7   7   7   7

shape the waist especially if being attached to a bodice

centre front

seam allowance

seam allowance

Dorota

top skirt

1970–1980

*

FROM ANDROGYNY TO JET SET

Profile portrait of Belgian-born American fashion designer Diane von Furstenberg. Von Furstenberg was one of the designers sought by the infamous jet set for their Studio 54 parties. Image 1977. Photograph by Susan Wood/Getty Images.

Pop musicians influenced fashion during the 1970s and their continuous raiding of the past allowed them to become the era's style makers. Bohemian dress became popular and the street trends of New York had a huge effect on fashion across the globe.

1970s

The 1970s were to be a come down from the high of the previous decade. The decade which had promised so much—the 1960s—had ended with personal tragedy and loss for many who had helped define the era. Brian Jones of the Rolling Stones had died of a drug overdose in 1969. This was followed closely by the deaths of Jimi Hendrix and Janis Joplin in 1970. Edie Sedgwick had also died of a drug overdose in 1971. Warhol's first superstar, Sedgwick, the original youth quaker, whose look was the inspiration to thousands, including John Galliano for Dior in the early 2000s, was the subject of the recent film *Factory Girl*, 2006.

The original queen of bohemia, Talitha Getty was also the victim of a fatal drug overdose in 1971. Getty deserves a special mention because, as an actress who had a small part in *Barbarella*, 1968, it was her marriage to Paul Getty and their home in Morocco that set the tone for bohemian lifestyle in the late 1960s. The bohemian style for Talitha had mainly been reinterpreted by Yves Saint Laurent, which is mirrored by Matthew Williamson reinterpreting the look for Sienna Miller in the new millennium. Saint Laurent was not the only designer to look at the concept of bohemian dress and aesthetic as inspiration. Other designers included Ossie Clarke, with his textile designer wife and Celia Birtwell, and their label Quorum, and Zandra Rhodes. These were the key figures for introducing the bohemian aesthetic to high fashion. Both these fashion houses relied on the use of colour and pattern printed on silk chiffon, a fabric which had not been popular brfore. The other event that signalled the end of the 1960s and a new order, was the murder of Sharon Tate. Tate was an American actress who had appeared in several films that highlighted her beauty. After receiving positive reviews for her performances, Tate was hailed as one of Hollywood's promising newcomers. Her fame increased after her marriage to film director Roman Polanski as did her appearances in fashion magazines as a model and cover girl. Tate was murdered, along with four others, in 1969 by the Mason Family— members of Charles Manson's quasi-commune. This event was to completely change the of behaviour of celebrity. No longer would stars be seen or accessible to fans and from this point onwards they would be surrounded by a bodyguard or minder. The looming safety spectre would be as much a part of the celebrity look as the oversized sunglasses which they still hide behind. Tate's murder was the defining moment when celebrities became aware that not all the attention from the public is that of adoration.

The early part of the decade saw the start of economic hardship which brought about a feeling of uncertainty as global recession set in. For many in the Western world the decade appeared to lurch from one economic problem to another: from the OPEC oil crisis in 1973 and the introduction of the three day week in the same year, to the 1978 Winter of Discontent. The beginning of 1979 saw the defeat of the Calaghan's Labour government and the rise of Thatcherism that would signify the economic boom of the 1980s.

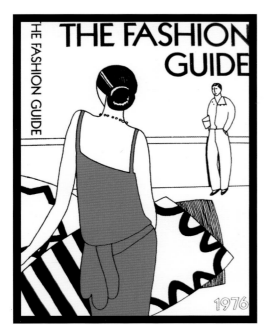

In times of recession and uncertainty there is often the urge and desire to look back to periods which appeared safer, more familiar and comfortable—the epitome of a golden age is that it is always retrospective—and this can be seen to have happened in the early 1970s. It was not only in fashion but also in film; as *Bonnie and Clyde*, 1967, starring Faye Dunaway and Warren Beatty, had started the whole notion of shopping for vintage or thrift shop culture. Film and fashion seemed to look back with a romantic longing and a highly idealised notion of the art deco period in the late 1920s and early 1930s. It was not that film or fashion focused on the everyday wardrobe of the period. It was the seemingly glamorised lives of the super rich that was depicted. Two films which explored the period, and in so doing created an attractive, idealised version of the era, were Roman Polanski's *China Town*, and *The Great Gatsby*, both in 1974. Bob Fosse's *Cabaret*, 1972, also made the 1920 to 1930 period a symbol of cool.

Previous Page The infamous Pop artist Andy Warhol, 1928–1987, sits next to actress Edie Sedgwick and lights her cigarette, on the set of one of his many films, 1965. Photograph by Walter Daran/Hulton Archive/Getty Images.

Opposite: Liza Minnelli, as Sally Bowles, in a scene from the film *Cabaret*, based on the Bob Fosse musical. The film is set in Berlin during the Weimar Republic, an era revered in the fashion of the 1970s. Photograph by Alan Pappe. Image courtesy Time Life Pictures, 1972.

Top Left: David Reeson illustration for *The Fashion Guide*, 1976. The style of the illustration clearly shows the retro art deco feel of the period.

Top Right: Bonnie Parker and Clyde Barrow, circa 1934. The two were notorious outlaws, robbers, and criminals who travelled across America robbing banks, small stores and gas stations.

BIBA

Left: The image for the launch for Big Biba based on silent movie stars of the 1920s.

Below: Biba outfit in brushed cotton from Big Biba, circa 1971.

Opposite: Biba halterneck jumpsuit, circa 1970. Ready-to-wear fashion before the start of the Biba era was mainly aimed at an older generation. As a result, most prices were too high for many younger buyers and the designs also were not aimed at their market. Biba set out to change this and bring fashion items to a wider market.

The afore mentioned Biba, a London label, was maybe the best example of the resurfacing of the 1930s aesthetic in the 1960s. Biba was the brainchild of Barbara Hulanicki and her husband Stephen Fitz-Simon. Hulanicki had originally worked as fashion illustrator for *Vogue* before winning an *Evening Standard* competition for a simple beachwear dress. The first Biba boutique opened in Abingdon Road in 1964 and then moved onto Kensington High Street, London, occupying the whole of the 1930s department store Derry and Toms. The garments were available to all through the catalogues which the fashion house produced. The images of the Biba catalogues— amongst the most iconic of the 1960s decade—had been created by legendary photographers such as Helmut Newton and the more recognisable Biba images were produced by Sarah Moon. Biba was the only department store to open after the Second World War and was one of the first that did not adopt the hard sell, leaving customers to explore the store unhindered by pushy assistants. Because of this, Hulanicki admits in her book *From A to Biba*, a great deal of stock left the store without going via the cash desk. Biba had an original and unique look, which morphed the pre-Raphaelite sensibility with the high glamour of the silent movie star.

Biba clothing was instantly recognisable, with high-cut sleeves. The colour palette was predominantly dark sludge shades in plum and brown and Biba used fabrics that had not been popular since the 1930s. Hulanicki claimed her inspiration had been the wardrobe of her glamorous aunt who she remembered from childhood. The look of Biba was 1930s influenced yet it was not a pastiche of the period as there was a more edgy, savvy and knowing feel to the designs and range of colours. Biba were the first cosmetic line to introduce black lipstick and nail varnish to their range, which they did under the name Posh Plum. Although a department store, Biba attracted a celebrity following including Marianne Faithfull, Cathy McGowan, David Bowie and Mick Jagger. The store provided the latest designs at affordable prices. Biba was even to give Anna Wintour, the current editor of *American Vogue*, her first job in fashion.

The influence of Hulanicki cannot be underestimated. She created the costumes for Julie Christie in the Oscar winning film *Darling*, 1965, and launched a cosmetic range that sold in 33 countries across the world at the height of its fame. The name still has a magic quality and there have been many attempts to relaunch the label without the artistic direction of Hulanicki, who left Britain for Brazil after the collapse of the company in the mid-1970s. Hulanicki re-emerged in America in the 1980s as an interior designer who breathed life back into Miami's 1930s beachfront architecture. The American designer, Anna Sui, was heavily influenced by her experience of Biba when she visited the store in the 1970s. From the colour palette Sui uses, to the shape of her perfume bottle, the impact of Biba on her work can be clearly felt.

BIBA CATSUIT

① Front

Bodice bagged out

Dorota

① Back

edge stitch inside

zip in centre back

Dorota

① Join bodice & trouser block to create catsuit block

Take in 1cm on side seams to avoid bagginess

lower crotch for a snugger fit

hipline   hipline

knee line   knee line

Dorota

② Draw style lines on new block shape

Dorota

③ final pattern pieces —

(add seam allowance)

(bodice is cut double)

cut 2 pairs   cup

back bodice   cut 2 pairs

cut 2

front bodice

cut 1   zip guard

cut 1 pair   cut 1 pair

back   front

Dorota

PATTERN PIECES FOR THE BIBA CATSUIT. THIS BIBA CREATION IS BEST MADE FROM A POLYESTER AND COTTON OR VISCOSE FABRIC ALLOWING THE FABRIC TO FLOW. THE CATSUIT IS NOT FOR THE FAINTHEARTED AND, IF FOLLOWING THESE PATTERN PIECES, THE WEARER NEEDS TO BE AT LEAST 5 FEET 10 INCHES TALL AND A BRITISH SIZE EIGHT. ILLUSTRATION BY DOROTA WOJCIECHOWSKA.

RED STRIPE TOMATO SUIT

ruffle front tie jacket

Back

Front

puff sleeve

front meet at centre front

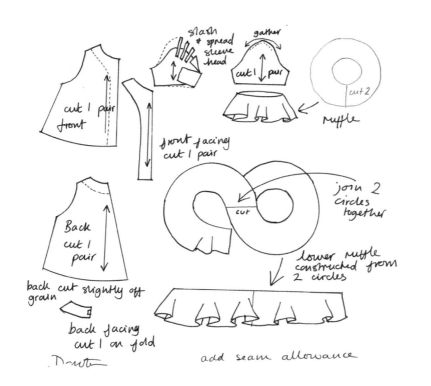

slash & spread sleeve head

gather

cut 1 pair

ruffle

cut 2

cut 1 pair front

front facing cut 1 pair

cut

join 2 circles together

Back cut 1 pair

lower ruffle constructed from 2 circles

back cut slightly off grain

back facing cut 1 on fold

add seam allowance

PATTERN PIECES FOR THE 1970s BIBA SUIT. CERTAINLY A GARMENT TO STAND OUT IN, THIS TOMATO PRINTED SUIT IS MADE FROM COTTON FLANNELETTE WHICH IS GENERALLY ASSOCIATED WITH BED LINEN. THE GARMENT HAS A VERY SPACIOUS CUT WITH RUFFLES MADE FROM FULL CIRCLES. ILLUSTRATION BY DOROTA WOJCIECHOWSKA. GARMENT COURTESY OF IAIN BROMLEY.

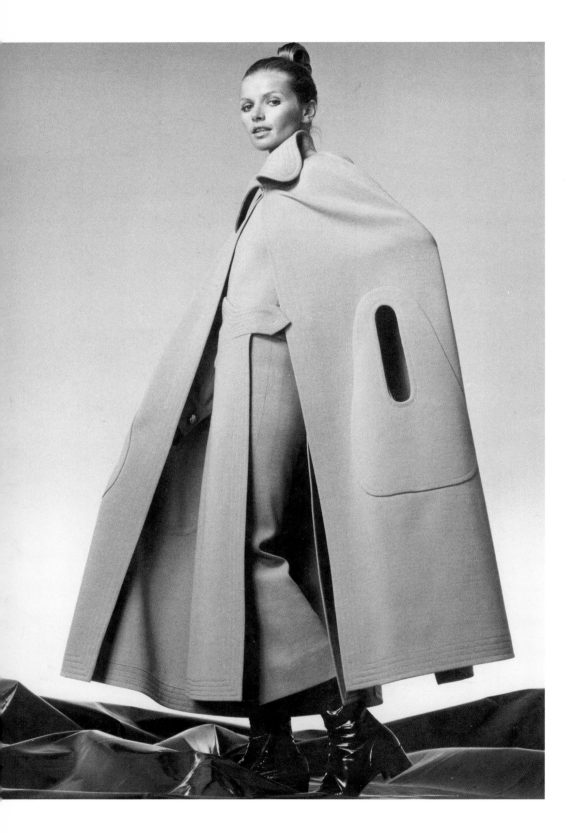

Through out the 1960s London had established itself as the home of youth culture and a source of creativity—a position it still maintains to the present day. In the 1960s there had been an explosion on the music scene of artists who were from all parts of Britain, from The Beatles in Liverpool to the Rolling Stones in London, and yet these bands had had a global impact on the youth market, not only in terms of sound but also look. London had become the centre of the youth fashions that had effected the world from the 1960s. This trend was to continue in the new decade with stores such as London's Big Biba, which was the first ever lifestyle store in Britain. Carnaby Street and King's Road, London, were the Meccas of youth style in the same way Newburgh Street would become the centre of new British talent in the 1980s.

Youth culture is made up of recognisable signs and symbols which those in the know, or with similar interests, respond to. Youth culture has often evolved as tribes or groups and this is depicted mainly by their dress and appearance, from the first teddy boys in the 1950s with their drapes, to the hip hop kids of the late 1990s with their low riding jeans and outsize sport clothing; a trend which has continued into the new millennium. In the 1970s there were youth fashions which did not just define themselves in terms of belonging to a subculture but also tackled the idea of sexuality and gender through dress. This is not to say that clothing did not previously express a gender but during the early part of the 1970s a de-gendering of clothing was evident. This gave people more freedom choice in their dress, resulting in greater self-expression through fashion.

A sharp, geometric cape and jumpsuit by Pierre Cardin, 1970. Known for his avant garde style and his space age designs, Cardin preferred geometric shapes and motifs, often ignoring the natural lines of the female form.

LIBERATION

The late 1960s had been a time of protest and revolution in the arena of social rights. America had brought the to the forefront issues such as the civil rights movement, decolonisation, women's liberation, gay and lesbian liberation, green and peace movements.

It was gay liberation and the decriminalisation of homosexuality in Britain in 1967 which can be viewed as a catalyst that brought about changes in dress in the early 1970s. Free from fear of prosecution or the feeling that careers could be halted with the wrong sort of media attention and gossip, male popstars such as David Bowie were able to explore the idea of gender through dress and invent intricate personas. Bowie morphed through personas Ziggy Stardust, Aladdin Sane and The Thin White Duke and his exploration of gender and sexuality through dress can be clearly seen in his album covers of the time. On the cover of *Hunky Dory*, 1972, Bowie strikes a pose which obviously refers to Greta Garbo and on the album art for *The Man Who Sold the World*, 1970, he reclines in a *chaise longue* with long hair and a dress. Bowie was to be a fashion and musical inspiration which lasted well into the next decade. Many of the leaders of new romantic movement and the, then termed, 'gender benders' (those who utilised their ambiguous gender and sexuality in their careers) such as Boy George, Marilyn and Pete Burns, give credit to Bowie for giving them the freedom to explore their own personas.

Women, such as Grace Jones, under the artistic direction of Jean Paul Goude, explored an androgyny reminiscent of Marlene Dietrich in the 1930s, but with a harder, sexier edge. Other female stars of the period also adopted a relaxed masculine dress sense which suited the decade amongst them were the actress Diane Keaton and singer/songwriter Patti Smith.

Singer and actress Grace Jones in 1974. Photograph by Robin Platzer. Image courtesy Time Life Pictures.

SEXUALITY

Popstars were not the only section of culture to play with the concept of androgyny in the 1970s. The British artist, Andrew Logan, launched the Alternative Miss World Competition in 1972, where predominantly male participants explored the idea of gender through costume. The first ever Alternative Miss World was held in the Rainbow Room at the Big Biba department store, London.

Displays of sexuality through dress was more conspicuous throughout the decade, not only with popstars pushing the boundaries on what was acceptable for different genders but in providing images which displayed high octane, overt sex appeal. Glam rock groups such as Roxy Music, with their costumes by Anthony Price, defined the era's cool in terms of sex appeal. Brian Ferry with his then girlfriend, the model Jerry Hall, defined the pinnacle of cool and sexy for the decade. This idea was put forward on many of Roxy Music's early album covers and their sexually suggestive titles. Seminal album, *For Your Pleasure*, features Amanda Lear walking a panther (signifying the predatory female, which was to be a popular theme when sexualising women in the next decade) and *Siren* depicts Jerry Hall as an alluring quasi-mermaid on the cover. Both of these women are dressed by Price.

Alternative Miss World, 1992.
Image courtesy Iain Bromley.

REBELLION

Fashion designers of the 1970s included Rudi Gernriech, 1922-1985, who explored the idea of gender through dress. Gernriech, an emigrate from Austria, had initially worked as a dancer until moving into fashion. Gernriech launched his label in the 1960s when youth and its meaning took on a new perspective on that which was conjured up in the 1950s. By the 1960s youth had come to represent the avant garde and in the 1970s it came to represent rebellion, especially in the hands of designers like Malcom MacClaren and Vivinne Westwood in the punk movement. Gernreich's work had been mainly in swimwear and underwear. He had introduced the unisex swimsuit and the monokini in the mid-1960s along with the flesh coloured body stocking. By the 1970s he was showing designs that totally hid the shape of the body and even the models hair had been shaved so as to play down any evidence of gender difference. This is the extreme of androgyny in fashion yet there is one staple item of clothing which is now completely unisex but in the late 1960s was a symbol of anti-fashion and protest wear—denim jeans.

Denim jeans had been staple American workwear from the late nineteenth century and worn by the farm workers and labourers—the career polar opposite of couture in the fashion spectrum. During the 1960s jeans, along with the poncho, became the clothing item that symbolised the protester. The actual ideology of denim being a symbol of disaffected youth was born in the 1950s with the stars Marlon Brando and James Dean. By the mid-1970s jeans were to pass from anti-fashion to high fashion as they became endowed with socialite and designer glamour. The Gloria Vanderbilt jeans by Murjani were the first designer pair. High-waisted and very tight, the Murjani jeans were made from dark blue stretch denim with gold stitching and the name of the New York socialite, Vanderbilt, on the back pocket. From here denim would never be the same again as other celebrities put their names to denim ranges, including the likes of Joan Collins. Fashion designers were also quick to launch their own brand of denim, the most famous being Calvin Klein who, with his advertising, had the teenage Brooke Shields in a state of undress telling us: "Nothing would come between me and my Calvins." By the early 1980s there was a huge choice in denim, from designer to branded. Levi's, who had been a market leader, saw its sales drastically drop over the period and relaunched themselves with the help of the London advertising agency Bartle, Bogle and Hegarty. Together they gave us the now infamous laundrette advert, which resulted in 501s being the brand leader and the only denim to wear in the 1980s.

Malcolm McLaren dressed head-to-toe in leather, 1976. McLaren was co-owner of the clothing shop Sex, London, with Vivienne Westwood. He was also manager of British punk band the Sex Pistols. The punk sensibilities can be seen in McLaren's clothing. Photograph by Express/Getty Images.

The idea of the socialite as designer, and the glamour they supposedly bestow onto the clothing, coincided with the birth of the jet set. The jet set could be defined as a group of international celebrities who were globally known. The group were at home anywhere from London, New York, Tokyo or Paris. They seemed unaffected by the economic crisis and life for them appeared to be one long party, depicted to the masses via the media. Members of this elite group came from all areas of culture including socialites and their rock star husbands (Bianca and Mick Jagger), artists (Andy Warhol), film stars (Liza Minnelli), fashion designers (Yves Saint Laurent and Halston) and models (Grace Jones and Jerry Hall). There were symbols that defined the jet set: their International fame, beauty and wealth; their ability to travel the globe preferably by Concorde (which had its first commercial flight in 1976) and their being seen to party at the famous club Studio 54. The jet set would be found wearing Yves Saint Laurent or Halston or one of the other key labels of the time like Fiorucci, Gucci and Zandra Rhodes.

THE JET SET

Studio 54 was the club to be seen at in the 1970s. Based just off Broadway at 254 West 54th street, New York, it was where the jet set and the beautiful people came to party and was to define the decade in terms of fashion excess and decadence. This indulgence coincided with the emergent punk scene in Britain as a reaction to the disengagement that many of the country's youth felt due to the continuing economic problems and their exclusion from society. Studio 54 opened in April 1977 as a joint venture by Steve Rubell and Ian Schrager. The club was huge not only in popularity and fame but in sheer size, complete with a stage and balcony area as the venue had originally been a 1920s theatre. The interior was very much left intact and the glamour and nostalgia was also seen in its iconic logo, designed by Gilbert Lesser, which had a distinctly art deco feel. Club nights at Studio 54 were infamous due to their excess which was often drug fuelled. One of the most infamous nights was in 1979 when Bianca Jagger, at her 30th birthday party, entered the club on a white horse. Jagger wore a white dress by the new British design team David and Elizabeth Emanuel.

Opposite: Bianca Jagger in the Studio 54 heyday, 1973. Photograph by Norman Eales.

Top Right: Zandra Rhodes jacket in cream and pink spiral shell print, 1971. The jacket drapes in curves because the underarm seams follow the lines dedicated by the print. The base of the jacket is gathered into the contained line of the edge quilting. Image ourtesy Zandra Rhodes. A donation of Dasha Shenkman in the name of her mother Belle Shenkman.

HALSTON

The designer, Roy Halston, 1932–1990, became a fashion legend
in the 1970s. Monotitled Halston, as he would become commonly
known to millions of women worldwide, was the preferred designer
to the jet set along with Yves Saint Laurent. Halston's clients
included Liza Minnelli, Angelica Houston, Elizabeth Taylor and even
British royalty: Princess Margaret. With his body skimming fashions
in silk jersey and use of ultra-suede, Halston defined sexy as cool
and slinky. Anyone who knows Halston's work will recognise that
Tom Ford cannibalised the New York designer's work in his 1990s
collections for Gucci.

Halston had initially trained as a milliner before moving into
fashion and was responsible for creating the pillbox hat worn
by Jackie Kennedy for the inauguration of her husband, John F
Kennedy, in the early 1960s. What made Halston famous was the
fact that he licensed himself through department store JC Penney
and thereby his designs were available to all women at all levels of
society. The designer was sacked from his own company because
of his increased unreliability due to drug abuse.

The name Halston still has a magic quality and there have been
a number of attempts to bring the label back, most notably in 1997
under the artistic direction of Randolph Duke Jaren and more
recently in 2007 with Marco Zanni, the first designer for Donatella
Versace taking the helm. For those in the know, Halston is a label to
collect and is easily wearable as can be seen in an episode of *Sex and the
City*, where Carrie Bradshaw wears vintage Halston, in homage
to Jackie Kennedy, in a storyline where she dates a politician.

Roy Halston and Bianca Jagger at
Jagger's birthday party, 1980. As an
iconic clothing designer of the 1970s
Halston's long bohemian-esque
dresses, and copies of his style,
were popular throughout the mid-
1970s. Photograph by Ron Galella.

1980 – 1990

*

FASHION
AS ART

The conception of the style title and its relevance to culture made a huge difference to the contemporary 1980s landscape. It is through these titles that most people still experience high fashion in their homes today. The promotion of idealised individual visions was pioneered by fashion houses, as runway shows started selling lifestyle dreams rather than dresses to consumers. The 1980s saw the emergence of intellectual concept design and the re-emerging influence of Japanese design in high fashion. The birth of style over substance—a massive shift in fashion history—was prevalent.

THE STYLE TITLE

The 1980s can be seen as the decade of style just as the 1970s were considered, perhaps wrongly, as the decade that style forgot. The style titles—magazines which featured current fashion trends—had been launched in the late 1970s with the magazine *Boulevard*. The publication soon folded and other more accessible titles, which were less politically motivated, including *The Face, i-D, Sky* and *Blitz*. The 1980s was the video age and through the media, fashion and style had a greater cultural value. To the youth in the street, these magazines, along with the emerging youth television, dictated the prevailing styles of the day.

Television, for the youth generation in Britain, was the brainchild of Janet Street Porter, who had been an early model for fashion designer Zandra Rhodes, and was now an influential producer for the newly emerging Channel 4. Television programmes *Network 7* (one of the first transmissions focused totally at a youth market) and *Def II*, along with *MTV*, provided a weekly fix of the latest fashion trends and in music: the look or style of the band was now almost more important than the sound.

Previous Page: One of the iconic fashion pieces by designer France Andrevie, circa 1983.

Opposite: Strong angular shapes were a dominant silhouette of the 1980s, especially in the style titles of the time. Women's makeup in the magazines was often graphic with well defined block eyebrows which gave a feel of androgyny to the model. Illustration courtesy of David Reeson.

Top: This Bellville Sassoon image from the 1980s depicts the clean crisp lines that were prevalent during the decade.

Top: 1980s snood headdress which was popular in the early part of the decade. Illustration courtesy of David Reeson.

Opposite: Mid-1980s fashion illustration which shows the clear influence that hairdresser Vidal Sassoon had on the youth market. The strong angular blunt cut bob with short fringe was a key look put forward the Sassoon design team. Illustration David Reeson.

NEW ROMANCE

Punk lost its political edge in the 1980s and morphed into new wave, this in turn was replaced by new romance. This youth movement referenced styles and looks from the eighteenth century, as seen in John Galliano's graduate collection, *Fallen Angels*, which was bought by the major fashion house, Browns, and showcased in its window. New romantic styles came from a wide range of sources including 1940s film noir and the dandy of the eighteenth century. The extravagant movement gave London club culture a new direction—often the costume being worn would become the total experience, rather than the night itself. During the 1980s new romantic style can be seen worn by Sean Young in the film *Blade Runner*, 1982, (opposite) and this street style was also to be adopted by high fashion publications of the period, especially *Vogue*, which showcased the work of photographers such as Paolo Reversi and Sheila Metzner. The work of these image makers had a soft and ethereal quality which suited the new romantic sensibility and their escapist clothing. For many, new romance allowed them to briefly escape the economic reality of Britain in recession.

Opposite: Sean Young's costume in the critically acclaimed *Blade Runner,* 1982, was based on new romantic sensibilities. Male new romantics often dressed in caricaturally androgynous clothing and wore cosmetics. Illustration Aaron Walker, 2008.

Left: British pop singer, Steve Strange, is best remembered as the frontman of the 1980s new romantic group Visage. His new romantic dress is displayed in its full glory here.

VIVINNE WESTWOOD

During the 1980s fashion designers raided art and past culture as they sought inspiration. Vivienne Westwood separated from Malcolm McClaren and now looked back to the eighteenth century for source material. She often lifted ideas directly from the paintings of artists like Fragonard, Bouche or Watteau. Westwood reworked the silhouette to give it a contemporary feel such as her mini-crini, the Boucher corset top, which was a direct lift of an eighteenth century pattern rendered in modern materials, and later still her *Toile de Jouy* print in the early 1990s. These styles were not intended for the mass market but an intellectual elite who understood the cultural reference points being explored. Westwood, along with Jean Paul Gaultier and John Galliano, lead the pack of designers who raided the past. Fashion no longer had a large enough client base to keep it economically viable but as couture fashion became more escapist, the shows entered the art realm, which sold the dream to the masses through the image rather than the product. This reaffirmed the elite position of the designer in the public consciousness as a maker of high art and the place of the diffusion line (a more wearable and affordable collection inspired by the original) was also established to meet demand. Label awareness developed throughout the 1980s as yuppie culture took hold and designers launched diffusion lines—such as Junior Gaultier, Westwood Red label and Polo by Ralph Lauren—to feed their lifestyle aspirations.

The detachment of the collections from mainstream fashion as it appeared on the high street led to another phenomenon—the rise of the supermodel. Linda Evangelista, Christy Turlington, Naomi Campbell, Tajana Patitz and Cindy Crawford were the modern equivalent of the silent film star, with an earning potential to match. Evangelista famously commented: "Christie and I won't get out of bed for less than 10,000 dollars." This comment was to be their undoing. By the beginning of the 1990s, the supermodel reign was over as designers became aware that the public paid the models more attention than they did the clothing but—this only highlights how detached high fashion was from the reality of many women's lives.

Vivienne Westood shirt with *Toile de Jouy* print, circa 1992. The pattern on the fabric is a reworking of the popular eighteenth century print.

The AIDS virus had first been detected in more cosmopolitan cities such as New York and San Francisco, but soon it became global. The virus caused many to rethink their social patterns of behaviour. This change in behavior affected their mode of dress, primarily in clubwear. Sex was now off limits and there was a renewed interest in sexualising the body through clothing and display, rather than semi-nudity. This sexual-but-clothed aspect transferred into high fashion and its effects were felt through the whole of society. There were a number of alternative fashions which had existed within subcultures and on the fringes of mainstream culture. They explored sexuality in a look-but-don't-touch manner where the materials used to make the garments emphasised the body's curves. The garments were often skintight and restrictive, leaving little to the imagination.

Fetishwear had started to move away from the obvious sex scene through the work of designers such as Vivienne Westwood—who used rubber as a material and adopted fetish symbolism into her designs from the early 1970s in her boutique, Sex, on King's Road, London. Other subcultures, mainly punk and goth, had also begun to appropriate fetish clothing into their look for different reasons. The punks wore Westwood's bondage trousers, or one of the many imitations, for its shock value and the goths for the sheer pleasure the clothing gave. Many goths were drawn to the iconic figures of Carolyn Jones as Morticia Adams in television programme *The Adams Family*, Yvonne De Carlo as Lily in *The Munsters* and Diana Rigg in the role of Mrs Peel in *The Avengers* for reference points.

FETISH

Diana Rigg, 1968. Pictured in a scene from the television series *The Avengers,* Rigg's character, Emma Peel, is tied to train tracks in her sexually alluring, ultra-feminine catsuit.

Certain materials and clothing items have sexual fetish overtones which had been understood for centuries in Western culture. *Venus in Furs* written by Von Sacher Masoch in the late nineteenth century is one of the early reference points. There was, however, a cultural shift in the 1980s as there was a genuine fear of actual sexual contact and sex became ritualised, expressed through dress. In Britain there was a well established underground of fetish societies and clothing designers such as John Sutcliffe, with his label AtomAge, produced contemporary literature and a line of rubber clothing.

The appropriation of fetish imagery and the growth of the fetish club scene in London in the decade can be viewed as evidence of the effect that AIDS had had on the population. Club nights such as the Sex Maniacs Ball and the Rubber Ball in London, Dressing for Pleasure in San Francisco and Euro Perv in Amsterdam brought fetishwear for many out of the bedroom and into the open. The growth in clothing as a form of sexuality and sexual expression was taken on by designers. This included young designers based at the newly opened Hyper Hyper store on Kensington High Street, London. The labels ranged from Pure Sex and Deadlier than the Male, to high fashion with the design aesthetic put forward by Thierry Mugler. This marriage of fetish and fashion did not stay on the fringes of culture but was a driving force of London clubland and youth culture. The fetish look rejuvenated London clubland with Kinky Gerlinki, which had been influenced by the Black Transvestite Vogueing nights in New York hosted by Susan Barsch. These club nights married high fashion looks and ideas to the sex scene and, in turn, inspired other clubnights around the country such as Flesh at the Hacendia early 1990s.

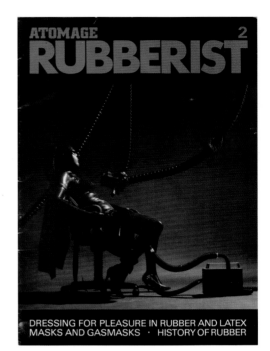

Opposite and Top: Front covers from *AtomAge* magazine, 1972. The fetish magazine was published in Britain by the designer John Sutcliffe as an offshoot of his AtomAge fetish clothing business. The first *AtomAge* clothing catalogue was published in 1965. The magazine specialised in leather, rubber and PVC fetishism, with a heavy emphasis on rubber and leather catsuits, cloaks, and gasmasks.

DECONSTRUCTION

The 1980s was also the time when the West had a renewed interest in Japanese design. The Japan aesthetic was just as new and radical in this period. This reiterated the influence of Japan on Western culture in the late nineteenth century when Japanese woodblocks inspired Impressionism.

The deconstruction movement in fashion heralded a new and exciting way of challenging existing aesthetics and silhouettes. This not only challenged visual sensibilities but also the philosophy effecting them. The entire endeavour was underpinned by the thinking and writing of Jacques Derrida, a highly regarded philosopher of contemporary culture. Designers associated with the deconstruction movement include: Rei Kawakubo for Comme des Garçons, Martin Margiela, Ann Demeulemeester and Dries van Noten. Designers challenged and brought fashion into perspective with other art forms such as architecture, graphic design and new media as well as contemporary literature and film theory. The designers acknowledged and celebrated the fact that clothing affects physical, cultural and ontological changes; allowing the wearer to celebrate the construction methods and create a new fashion *zeitgeist*.[1] Fashion design took on a social mantel again, being a social commentator and embracing the notion that fashion is actively synthesing not only visual influences, but cultural and political ones too. This theory is still reminiscent on today's catwalks.

The term deconstruction did not truly enter the fashion vernacular until the 1980s and has now become a key term. The actual word deconstruct sounds aggressive, industrial and even subversive in relation to fashion. The key designers already mentioned not only challenged pre-existing norms, but proactively broke conventions of construction methods and silhouette creation.

Unlike Dior's hour glass New Look, deconstructive designers actively used the body's shape as a basis, which was to have its proportions and curves re-aligned. In particular Rei Kawakubo, Issey Miyake and Yohji Yamamoto utilised their own cultural sensibility and the Eastern concept of symmetry (asymmetric balance) to produce a whole new aesthetic. They used and continue to use traditional draping and construction methods to create shapes which act in an opposite manner to the body form. Up until the deconstruction movement construction methods in fashion were internal. The processes in clothing manufacture were not to be celebrated and certainly not used for adornment. Deconstruction actively embraced this aspect, creating a whole new aesthetic showing and utilising these process methods as an integral part of the design and decoration.

Deconstruction garments challenged their ability to be worn. A key design feature for Comme des Garçons and Yohji Yamamoto has been to allow the wearer to interpret the garments as they wish; some of which can be worn in more than one way, for example upside down or back to front. The wearer arguably becomes as important as the designer and is allowed to personalise their look, stamping their own identity onto the garment.

Fabrics became an integral part of the innovation, many of them possessing new properties and being able to be used in new and creative ways—eg. fabrics can be molded or heat-sealed. Many bonded fabrics allow the designer to actively use the construction properties as part of their design.[2] With the synthesis of fabric and construction and design philosophy many of these garments stand alone as wearable sculptures.

[1] Alison, G, *Deconstruction Fashion: The Making of Unfinished, Decomposing and Re-assembled Clothes*, New York: Berg, 1998.
[2] Bonded fabric is fabric consisting of more than one layer 'fused' together or innovative new fabrics such as velvet and plastic.

COMME DES GARÇONS

Rei Kawakubo was born in Tokyo, 1942. Educated in fine art at the Keio University Tokyo. Graduating in 1964, she launched the Comme des Garçons label in Japan in 1969. Kawakubo made an indelible impression on Paris in the early 1980s with ripped and knotted fabrics, somber colours and asymmetrical detailing. Kawakubo has said of her own work:

> What I do is not influenced by what has happened in fashion or culture. I work from obscure abstract images to create a fresh concept of beauty. What the Japanese designers are doing is alien to us at the moment. But it is as liberating to wear as the Chanel suit must have been in the 1920s and look what happened to that.[3]

Kawakubo introduced the particular use of fabric to the fashion world. The collection showed others what was previously only seen by the wearer—the construction and interior of the garment. Kawakubo started from the early 1980s deconstructing and reassembling clothing to create a new aesthetic and feminine sensuality. Some of Kawakubo's past garments required diagrams as an explanation of how to put them on; for example some were produced with three sleeves or were two totally different styles joined together at the hem. Her challenging aesthetic has taken a while to be understood, but the challenge of, 'Body meets dress; dress meets body' was and still is enjoyed universally by wearers.

[3] Garner, L, *Daily Mail*, 27 March 1983.

Previous Page: Blue Yohji Yamamoto jacket, circa 1990. The garment is made form nylon and polyurethane, normally associated with wetsuits.

Opposite Left: Combination jacket of velvet, cotton and lace, circa 1990.

Opposite Right: Crumbled shirt, Robe de Chambre for Comme des Garçons, 1990.

All garments borrowed from by Val Furphy. Photographed by Iain Bromley.

1990–2000

*

FROM DECONSTRUCTION TO FASHION FUSION

It is important to look at where fashion is situated in a social and economic sense during the 1990s so that there can be insight to the vintage trends of the future. The main movers and shakers of the 1990s will inevitably become the vintage labels to watch out for as their couture collections, some with very limited runs, become extremely sought after. The pioneering aesthetic championed by the infamous Antwerp Six—a design collective which became infamous in the 1990s with their reworking of how fashion is viewed—will almost certainly become a design classic of the future.

1990s

The reinvention of many styles from previous decades was the main characteristic of the 1990s. The denim trend which originated in the 1960s, became increasingly adopted as the fabric of choice for casualwear. Denim was available in non-traditional colours such as pink, green and black, also on offer were different fabric washes such as stonewash, acid wash, dark wash and distressed denim.

Interestingly, the 1990s emergence of more challenging fashion came at a time when art itself is became less conformist. Artists such as Tracey Emin and Damien Hurst deconstructed art and the parallel in fashion was quite literal. Where fashion showed the internal machinations of garments, art depicted the exposed internal organs of animals. Artists and designers in the 1990s were questioning the conventions of the aesthetics in their own disciplines. This not being a turgid reaction to creating an new philosophy but creating an antidote to the previous styles. An important fashion direction came from Antwerp, where designers explored new directions.

Previous Page: Gareth Pugh's designs reference the long tradition of fashion as performance art that stretches back through Alexander McQueen, John Galliano, and Vivienne Westwood to the 1980s club culture with fashion icon, Leigh Bowery.

Left: Original Wonderbra advertising from 1975.

Opposite: The Spice Girls attending the 1997 MTV Video Awards in New York. Their look defined fashion for legions of girls in the 1990s. From left to right: Victoria Adams (now Beckham), Geri Halliwell, Melanie Brown, Emma Bunton and Melanie Chislom.

THE EARLY 1990s

The grunge style, which originated in Seattle, in America, was beginning to make itself known on the international scene in the 1990s. The look identified itself with stone washed jeans, lumberjack shirts and floral skirts or dresses worn with Converse boots or Doc Martins. Other revivals of fashions from the 1970s included bellbottomed trousers and flares, tie-dye t-shirts, and waistcoats with fringes. Body adornment such as piercings and tattoos became increasingly acceptable and were accentuated by belly tops. This body modification was not necessarily representative of a subculture but purely for self-adornment.

Designers such as Gianni Versace and Dolce and Gabbana were also designing in opposition to the sloppy styles, offering the female customer colourful feminine lines. Corsets and platforms re-emerged and were part of the fashion palette again. Similarly to previous decades, music influenced style.

Hip hop emerged in the 1990s, with a fashion of huge baggy trousers and sports clothing accessorised with baseball caps. The style was strong, characterised by oversized jerseys, neon tracksuits, and hightops, along with running shoes like Air Jordan, Reebok, and Adidas. Many designers began working in athleticwear, such as Ralph Lauren, Donna Karen, and Tommy Hilfiger, began to produce sports-inspired streetwear. Logos were popular and added perceived value to the garments. Logos in their own right became a fashion accessory.

With the eclecticism on offer and the more relaxed approach to fashion, other lifestyle choices were effecting fashion directions. New minimalist solutions were being explored such as the recycling of clothing. In 1993 two American designers, George Hansen and Susan Deputy, promoted a new trend towards making garments out of old pieces of clothing. This is also an idea which is embraced by Junky Styling in London who are now accepted as a directional label entering the arena of London Fashion Week. Indeed even Oxfam at one point reworked garments to be resold, although in their case it was not as profitable.

British pop music duo Bros, consisting of twin brothers Matt and Luke Goss, 1990. The pair wears the stonewashed denim that filled the early 1990s market. Photograph by Dave Hogan.

Image from the Walter van Beirendonck Autumn/Winter collection, 2007.

ANTWERP SIX

The Antwerp Six refers to a group of avant garde designers who graduated from Antwerp's Royal Academy of Fine Arts between 1980–1982, where they were taught by Linda Loppa. The group first established itself in 1988 when they rented a truck and, with their collections, travelled to London. Most of the six broke away from the group and, through the 1990s, started establishing themselves as inspirational designers in their own right. Paris, London, New York and Milan now have a new genre of creative designers who challenge pre-ordained fashion principles. The Antwerp Six's distinctive look fits into the deconstructive mould in that they are challenging silhouettes; although their shapes are harder than Japanese silhouettes and they play more actively with colour, graphics and fabrics.

WALTER VAN BEIRENDONCK

Born in Brecht, 1957, Walter van Beirendonck graduated from the Royal Arts Academy in Antwerp. His fellow graduating classmates in 1981 were Dirk van Saene, Dries van Noten, Ann Demeulemeester and Marina Yee. From 1983 van Beirendonck has worked on his own collections, which are inspired by literature, visual arts, nature and travel. In 1997 he designed the costumes for U2's PopMart tour and, in 1999, was awarded the honorary title of Cultural Ambassador of Flanders: his hometown. In 2001 he was the curator for the exhibition *Mode 2001* in Antwerp.

DRIES VAN NOTEN

Belgium born Dries van Noten had his first menswear collection in London with the other designers from the Antwerp Six. He produces four collections a year including menswear, womenswear and childrenswear. Van Noten's work is characterised by the innovative use of prints, colours, original fabrics and layering. His first shop, Het Modepaleis, opened in Antwerp in 1989 and van Noten now has several outlets. In 2008 van Noten won the prestigious International Award of the Council of Fashion Designers of America.

DIRK BIKKEMBERGS

Born in Cologne, Germany, Dirk Bikkembergs was initially interested in studying law. Having changed his mind Bikkembergs graduated from the Royal Academy in 1982 and, in 1985, won the Canette d'Or award for best designer in fashion. Later that same year Bikkembergs created his own mens shoe collection and a complete menswear collection was launched in 1989 in Paris. His influences include the military and he loves simple shapes and enduring materials, which include leather.

MARINA YEE

Marina Yee launched her first womenswear collection in 2003 and moved away from the regular fashion produced by her counterparts. Yee creates installations, which include video and other contemporary mediums. One of the keen supporters of group Beauty Without Irony, Yee's work plays with the senses and sheds light on every day objects, which discover a new aesthetic.

DIRK VAN SAENE

After graduation Dirk van Saene opened the small shop, Beauties and Heroes, selling his own homemade clothes. In 1983 he won the gold award at Belgium's prestigious Golden Spindle contest. In 1990, van Saene launched his first catwalk show in Paris. He draws on many influences for his work including inspiration from fine arts, citing work of Louise Bourgeois and Ellsworth Kelly as inspiration. In 2001 van Saene curated an exhibition in Antwerp part of the fashion project entitled Mode-Landed.

ANN DEMEULEMEESTER

Born in Kortrijk, Belgium, in 1959 Ann Demeulemeester's first ready-to-wear collection was produced in 1981 and in 1985 she founded the company 32 with her husband. Demeulemeester's garments have an edgy avant garde element, which include different fabrics, slashes, and rips and are manufactured in a sombre colour palette of browns, greys and blacks. She is known for her slouchy masculine look, which has become her signature referencing her longtime muse Patti Smith. Claudia Schiffer is also wore a Demeulemeester shirt on the cover of *Vogue*, July 1996, extending her endorsement to a wider audience.

MARTIN MARGIELA

Although Martin Margiela was not part of the Antwerp Six, he too graduated from the Royal Academy of Fine Arts in Antwerp and has been an inspirational designer in his own right. Margiela was born in Belgium, in 1959, and is closely associated with the deconstructionist fashion movement of the 1980s. Margiela's work is characterised by a poetic appreciation of imperfection, personality and eccentricity. His collections have been presented on tube platforms and street corners. He says: "My main inspiration has always has been the extremities and changes of daily life". Margiela, produces very limited runs of his pieces—maybe only eight items per batch. The idea of being unique is clearly where Margiela has established a niche market utilising Aristsanal vintage clothes. Garments from the past are reworked, for example a nineteenth century huntsman's waistcoat, to create a customised and very individual, desirable piece.

A model walks down the catwalk during the Martin Margiela fashion show as part of Paris Fashion Week Spring/Summer 2007. Photograph by Karl Prouse for Catwalking.com. Image courtesy Getty Images.

SKATERS, PREPS AND GIRL POWER

The late 1990s continued the sportswear theme, introducing the skateboarding style, especially raising the profile of skate shoes which, once they reached mainstream, were high in demand. Hoodies and baggy jeans—fashion garments synonymous with skaters—were again popular during this period.

Fashion styles throughout the decade were influenced by sportswear and utilitywear. The preppy style of dress was actually influenced by the surfing culture of California and Hawaii. Cargo trousers, (originally found on army clothing) and faded denim were styled with polo shirts and t-shirts with surf-inspired graphics. Designers too were influenced by this new phenomena of remodelling sportswear. This included Junior Gaultier introducing platform trainers, Junya Watanabe designing for Fred Perry, Stella McCartney for Adidas and Alexander McQueen for Puma.

Girl Power became a phenomenal force in the 1990s, which was encapsulated by the hugely successful band Spice Girls. The band were a cultural phenomenon and shaped mainstream society and culture endorsing everything from dolls to deodorant and crisps. Again the look for this market was an eclectic style with many elements gathered from the previous decades. Differing from other manufactured bands, each Spice Girl had her own style. The platform trainers, similar to those made by Junior Gaultier, were a staple of their wardrobes. Spice Girl Victoria Beckham, now a fashion phenomenon in her own right, favoured Gucci and latterly designers such as Cavali, thus fuelling her nickname of Posh Spice.

The preppy 1990s styles are displayed here by the *Beverly Hills 90210* cast, 1995. Clockwise from bottom left: Brian Austin Green, Tiffani-Amber Thiessen, Luke Perry, Gabrielle Carteris, Mark Espinoza, Jason Priestley, Ian Ziering, Tori Spelling and Jennie Garth. Photograph by Fox Broadcasting/Getty Images.

FUTURE TRENDS

Fashion is collaborating with other creative discipline thus enriching and widening its appeal and interpretation. Fashion is no longer the pursuit of celebrities and the rich; it has a place for every wearer. Vintage, as a term, is a much more exclusive as opposed to secondhand. It is conceivable that in the short term future, Britain will have the giant thrift shops and warehouses currently found in America and Germany. The vintage fashion fairs are slowly moving towards this, but as present have a nomadic existence which strives for permanency.

Fashion is moving in and collaborating in different arenas, as can be seen from some of the work featured in this chapter. Cross-pollination and collaborative approach enable fashion to become an art form in its own right. It has a place as an installation, as an interactive and virtual experience, a gallery space or a film.

Designers are reaching another audience. Samsung's collaboration with Armani for example, Prada with LG Mobile and Hussein Chalayan with the electronics chain Philips. The designer's touch is creating a luxury-inspired item which is being purchased by a wider audience than that of the fashion conscious wearer. This collaboration means designers are creating more than dreams; they are creating lifestyle experiences which are thought provoking and can be termed as intellectual design. Preconceived norms are challenged and the avant garde is reborn.

New York is evolving as a centre of avant garde fashion which had up to this point been the bastion of Paris, Tokyo, London and Antwerp. New York has a sound reputation for commercial ready-to-wear. The academic, Peter Burger, defined avant garde as, "the place of political engagement in art".[4] Some of the influential designers coming out of New York include: Slow and Steady Wins the Race, Tess Giberson, Three As Four and Miguel Adrover. These designers offer another design ethos in contrast to the mainstream, where they explore unusual construction and silhouettes. Slow and Steady Wins the Race, for example, investigates seams and construction, whereas Three as Four challenge silhouettes and the mainstream manufacturing techniques. Slow and Steady Wins the Race shows sports seaming techniques on structured garments, again giving a deconstructed feel.

[4] Burger, P, *Theory of the Avant Garde*, Chicago, 1984.

An image from the Hussein Chalayan Autumn/Winter 2003 womenswear collection named Kinship Journeys. Photograph Chris Moore, 2003.

INNOVATION

Innovative silhouettes are still a key aspect of fashion design with many designers such as Viktor & Rolf, Boudicca and Gareth Pugh. These designers constantly evoke a sense of drama, using art and theatre as a reference point. Art galleries and museums, rather than the high end fashion buyer, are becoming the audience, thus the fashion is being elevated to an art form, entering a new arena.

Fabric innovation was, and is, influencing trends and lifestyle are the inclusion of spray on fabrics, glue-based fabrics and those containing scent. Techno fabrics and bonded fabrics which change with colour are being increasingly introduced into mainstream fashion. Technology is being worn as an accessory—for example garments often include hidden pockets for MP3 players. Technology and connectivity progress at an alarming rate while personal handheld technology like mobile phones became smaller. Technology within fabrics is still innovating with ventures such as spray on fabrics and scent garments, affording the wearer to have a unique garment suited to them.

Technology and innovation are entering a new collaboration and allowing the wearer to, in effect, became the designer by selecting their own variants to create something unique. Consumers are becoming more conscious of external factor affecting fashion such as the emergence of Fair Trade and an awareness of ethical and sustainable fashion which marries well with the notion of vintage—in the sense of recycling garments.

In essence through this exploration characterizes that design autonomy is being handed to the wearer; here Individuals are able to develop their own identities. It is quite acceptable to blend vintage and retro with current designer and high street items thus creating an eclectic visual mixture.

Opposite: Scentsory Design by Dr Jenny Tillotson, PhD from the Royal College of Art, currently a senior research fellow in the sensory, aroma and medical field in fashion and textiles at Central Saint Martins College of Art and Design. Fabrics and garments can be affected by our moods and needs. Image circa 2007.

Left and Right: Gareth Pugh designs from the early collection referencing the long tradition of fashion as performance art.

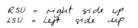
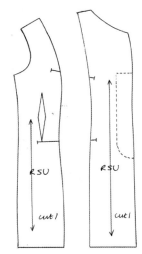
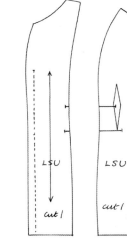
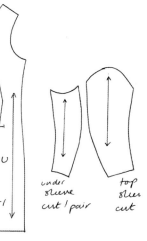

RSU

cut 1

RSU

cut 1

LSU

cut 1

LSU

cut 1

under
sleeve
cut 1 pair

top
sleeve
cut

PAUL SMITH'S TEDDY BOY
DRAPE-INSPIRED JACKET.
THE JACKET SHOULD BE
MADE FROM LIGHTWEIGHT
WOOL FOR EASY DRAPE.
THE GARMENT ALSO HAS
THE OPTION OF A VENT IN
THE BACK AND CONCEALED
BUTTON FASTENING.
INTRICATE HANDFINISHING
ON COLLAR AND REVER
AND PLACKET AND POCKET
DETAILING AT FRONT. THE
JACKET FINISHES THREE-
QUARTERS OF THE WAY DOWN
THE LEG, DESIGNED TO
BE WORN WITH CIGARETTE
TROUSERS AND VERY HIGH
HEELS. ILLUSTRATION BY
DOROTA WOJCIECHOWSKA.

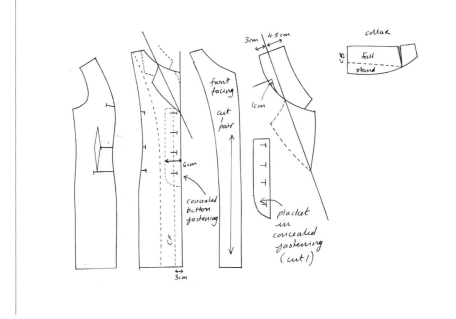

front
facing

cut
pair

concealed
button
fastening

CF

3cm

3cm 4.5cm

1cm

placket
in
concealed
fastening
(cut 1)

collar

CB

fall

stand

OWNING VINTAGE GARMENTS

ACCESSORIES

There are many purists in the realm of vintage fashion. They believe that when investing in vintage garments, one should concentrate on a particular era and never confuse decades in a singular collection. However when collecting vintage fashion, the continuous adding of personal touches and flourishes and
constantly playing with silhouettes and eras creates a very individual, eclectic look.

Whatever era you chose, the garments can be accessorised with period or contemporary pieces, giving a look a much fresher, eclectic and modern feel. This is the epitome of past meeting present in a singular look. Depending on the desired effect it is important to be aware that combining a variety of materials, such as plastics, glass, ivory or shell, creates a conflict in textures and luminosity. A dress with pearls may not necessarily work with glass bangles. Sometimes creating a strong visual by juxtaposing elements is exactly what is desired. It is always important to experiment.

CUSTOMISATION

Essentially, purists believe that vintage garments should not be modified. However some modifications may have taken place a few decades ago, still strangely enough becoming vintage in themselves. Some garments have been repaired or altered and in these cases it is best to assess the quality of the fabric or the trims. In some instances these trims become collectable and expensive in their own right. It has been reported that customers have bought Chanel jackets for the gold chains in their hems.

LOOKING AFTER VINTAGE GARMENTS

The main thing to remember is that vintage clothing, by its very nature, is old and should be treated with care. With any garment, fibres can become unstable and disintegrate over time and pigments may become unstable, fading or transferring onto other surfaces. It is important to keep vintage garments away from direct sunlight and extreme temperatures.

Depending on the type of garment, it should be either hung up in a suit-carrier, a folded in a box with acid free tissue paper or hung carefully on padded hangers to stop pulling and stretching of the fabric. If the garment is in a suit-carrier, it is still important to place tissue into certain shapes, for example puff sleeves, in order to keep their shape.

Ensure the garment is hanging up with enough space around it so as not to incur any creasing.

Knitwear may not necessarily keep well if hung up and may stretch. In this case box storage with ample tissue is often the most appropriate method for storage. In some cases, garments should be handeled with gloves.

It is important to be mindful of ethical and sustainable issues relating to vintage clothing. Many garments incorporate animal byproducts such as fur and ivory, so before investing ensure you are truly aware of the materials used.

Other factors affecting caring for the garments include the direct materials the trims are produced in, these include:

Ivory
Mother of pearl
Shells
Pearls
Fur
Feathers
Leather and suede
Metal
Glass
Plastic
Hair

Each of the following materials need to be specially cleaned in order for the garments to retain as much quality as possible during its life.

		Detergent/ cleaning product
Ivory	Cloth and warm water	No
Mother of Pearl	Cloth and warm water	No
Shell	Cloth and warm water	No
Pearls	Cloth and warm water	No
Fur	Gentle brush	No
Feathers	Gentle brush	No
Leather and suede	Cloth and warm water	Mild cleaner
Metal	Cloth and warm water	Mild cleaner
Glass	Cloth and warm water	Mild cleaner
Plastic	Cloth and warm water	Mild cleaner
Hair	Dust clean	No

REMEMBER

Do not put the garments into a washing machine. Sometimes sponging stains maybe adequate, test on an area not readily visible.

Use professional cleaners, check the type of treatment they require.

Check whether trims need to be removed and whether buttons need to be covered before any treatment with chemicals.

Be aware that some garments will disintegrate upon contact with cleaning solutions.

Different fibres react differently in water, check if possible the fibre content of the fabric and thread stockists.

Christian Dior's couture collection from 1973 which epitomise the look and feel of the era.

BRITISH AND AMERICAN STOCKISTS

AUCTIONS

Bonhams
www.bonhams.com

Christies
www.christies.com

Phillips
www.phillips-auctions.com

Sotheby's
www.sothebys.com

William Doyle Galleries
www.doylenewyork.com

MARKETS

Bermondsey Market
London Bridge, London.

Camden Market
www.camdenlock.net

Camden Passage
www.camdenpassageislington.
co.uk

Greenwich Market
www.greenwichmarket.net

Thrift shops and flea markets in New
York
www.allny.com/thrift.html

Hell's Kitchen Flea Market
www.hellskitchenfleamarket.com

Portobello Market
Portobello Road, Ladbroke
Grove End, London.
www.portobelloroad.co.uk

Spitalfields Market
Liverpool Street, London.
www.visitspitalfields.com

WEBSITES

3rd And 56th Street
www.3rdand56thstreetclothi
ng.co.uk

Absolute Vintage
www.absolutevintage.co.uk

American Vintage Blues
www.vintageblues.com

American Vintage Classics
www.americanvintage
classics.com

Another Time Vintage Apparel
www.nothertimevintage
apparel.com

Antique and Vintage Clothing
www.antiquedress.com

Atom Retro
www.atomretro.com

Beyond Retro
www.beyondretro.com

Biba Lives Vintage Clothing
www.bibalives.com

Blue Velvet Vintage
www.bluevelvetvintage.com

Bobby Dene
www.bobbydene.com

Bramble Designs Ltd
www.brambledesigns.com

Buffalo Gal Vintage
www.buffalogalvintage.com

Cad van Swankster Men's
Vintage Clothing
www.thegirlcanthelpit.com

Cenci Vintage Clothing and
Accessories
www.cenci.co.uk

Circa Vintage
www.circavintage.com
Contentment Farm
www.
contentmentfarmantiques.com

The Contemporary Wardrobe
www.contemporarywardrobe.
com

Cutler and Gross Vintage
www.cutlerandgross.com/
vk_vintage_index.htm

Dolly Diamond Vintage
Fashion
www.dollydiamond.com

Enchanted Oldies
www.enchanted-oldiesvintage.com

Everything Queer
www.everythingqueer.co.uk
Fever Vintage
www.fevervintage.com

The Frock
www.thefrock.com

Gadabout Vintage
www.gadaboutvintage.com

The Girl Can't Help It
www.alfiesantiques.com

Hemlock Vintage Clothing
www.hemlockvintage.com

Hornets Men's Vintage
Clothing
www.hornetskensington.co.uk

Jill Barron aka Butterfly Girl
www.butterflygirl.com

Karen Augusta
Antique Lace and Fashion
www.antique-fashion.com

Kazmattazz Ltd
www.kazmattazz.com

Kingston Antiques
www.kingstonantiquesmarket.
co.uk

Lace Guild
www.laceguild.demon.co.uk

The Lace Museum
www.thelacemuseum.org

The Master Cleaners
www.themastercleaners.com

Meg Andrews
Antique Costumes and
Textiles: Collectable, Hangable,
Wearable.
www.meg-andrews.com

Monster Vintage
www.monstervintage.com

Mystique Vintage Clothing and
Accessories
www.mystiquevintage.com

Neon Womb
Punk and Gothic Clothing
www.neonwomb.com

New Kings Road Vintage
Guitar Emporium
www.newkingsroadguitars.
co.uk

P and A Antiques Ltd
www.pa-antiques.co.uk

Paisley Babylon
www.paisleybabylon.com

Past Patterns
www.pastpatterns.com

Prettypetticoat Ltd
www.prettypetticoat.com

Radio Days
www.radiodaysvintage.co.uk

Rapanui Clothing
www.rapanuiclothing.com

Red Light Vintage Clothing
www.redlightvintage.com

Rewind Vintage
www.rewindminneapolis.com

Ribbons and Taylor Vintage
Clothing
www.ribbonsandtaylor.co.uk

Rokit
www.rokit.co.uk

Rusty Zipper
www.rustyzipper.com

Sydney Vintage
www.sydneys-vintage-clothing.
blogspot.com

The Swing Bunch
www.theswingbunch.co.uk

Tangerine Boutique
Early Vintage, Antique and
Period Clothing
www.tangerineboutique.com/
pre1950.htm

Tin Tin Collectibles, Alfies
Antique Market
www.tintincollectables.net

Unique Vintage
www.unique-vintage.com

Victorian Elegance
www.victorianelegance.com

Vintage American Clothing
www.vintageamericanclothing.
com

Vintage City Clothing
www.vintagecityclothing.com

The Vintage Clothing Company
www.vintageclothingcompany.com

Vintage Fashion Guild
www.vintagefashionguild.org

Vintage in Style
www.vintage-instyle.com

Vintage Knits
www.vintageknits.com

Vintage Magazine Shop
www.vinmag.com

Vintage Martini
www.vintagemartini.com/
clothinglinks.html

Vintage Modes
www.vintagemodes.co.uk

Vintage Textile
www.vintagetextile.com

Vintage Vixen
www.vintagevixen.com

Vintageous
www.vintageous.com

Viva Vintage
www.vivavintageclothing.com

Woodland Farms Antiques
www.woodlandfarmsantiques.
com/enter.html

1960s miniskirt and pageboy hat.
Illustration by Charlotte Craig, 2008.

BIBLIOGRAPHY

FASHION AND ART

Biennale di Firenze, DAP Skira editore, 1997.

Clark, O, *The Ossie Clark Diaries*, Lady Henrietta Rous ed, Lomdon: Bloomsbury, 1998.

Drake, N, *The 1950s in Vogue*, New York: Conde Naste Publications Ltd, 1987.

Gorman, P, *The Look: Adventuress in pop and rock Fashion*, foreword by Malcolm McLaren, London: Sanctuary Publishing Ltd, 2001.

Kylie, London: V&A Publications in association with the Arts Centre Melbourne, Australia, 2005.

Leon Talley, A, *Diane von Furstenberg: The Wrap*, New York: Assouline Publishing, 2004.

Mauries, P, *Christian Lacroix: The Diary of a Collection,* London: Thames and Hudson, 1996.

Readers Digest. *Journeys into the Past: Life on the Home Front,* London: Readers Digest Association Ltd, 1993.

Rennolds-Milbank, C, *New York Fashion: the Evolution of American Style,* New York: Abrams Inc Publishers, 1989.

Stanfill, S, *New York Fashion,* London: V&A Publications, 2007.

Various, *Fashion People,* New York: Assouline Publishing, 2003.

PATTERN CUTTING BOOKS

Bray, N, *Dress Fitting,* London: Wiley Blackwell, 1992.

Cabrera, R and Meyers, P, *Classic Tailoring Techniques: A Construction Guide For Womenswear*, London: Fairchild Books, 1986.

Campbell, H, *Designing Patterns: a Fresh Approach to Pattern Cutting*, London: Nelson Thonres, 1980.

Cloake, D, *Fashion Design on the Stand*, London: Batford Ltd, 1996.

Gross, L, Kopp, E, Rolfo, V and Zelin, B, *Designing Apparel through the Flat Pattern*, London: Fairchild Books, 1992.

Gross, L, Kopp, E, Rolfo, V and Zelin, B, *How to Draft Basic Patterns*, London: Fairchild Books, 1991.

Holman, G, *Bias Cut Dressmaking*, London: Batsford, BT Ltd, 2001.

Joseph-Armstrong, H, *Draping for Apparel*, London: Fairchild Books, 2000.

Marshall, J, *Make Your Own Japanese Clothes*, New York: Kodansha International Ltd, 1995.

Mooney, S, *Making Latex Clothes*, London: Batsford, 2004.

Richardson, K, *Stretch Fashion: Design For Stretch and Knit Fabrics*, London Fairchild, 2008.

Shoben, M and Ward, J, *Patterns Cutting and Makiing Up. Vol. 2: The Simple Approach to Soft Tailoring (Revised Edition)*, London: London College of Fashion Media, 2000.

HISTORIC

Countryman, R and Weiss-Hopper, E, *Womenswear of the 1920s*, London: Players Press, 1998.

Countryman, R and Weiss-Hopper, E, *Womenswear of the 1930s*, London: Players Press, 2002.

Gordon, S, *Turn of the Century Fashion Patterns and Tailoring Techniques*, London: Dover Publications Inc, 2000.

Grimble, F, *After a Fashion: How To Reproduce, Restore and Wear Vintage Styles*, London: Lavolta Press, 1993.

Grimble, F, *The Edwardian Modiste: 85 Authentic Patterns*, London: Lavolta Press, 1997.

Sehep, RL, *The Great War: Styles and Patterns of the 1910s*, London: Players Press, 1998.

Harris, K, *59 Authentic Turn of fhe Century Fashion Patterns*, London: Dover Publications Inc, 1994.

Harris, K, *Authentic Victorian Dressmaking Techniques*, London: Dover Publications, 1999.

Ralston, M, *Fashion Outlines: Dress Cutting by the Block Pattern System*, London: Lacis Publishing, 1990.

Shep, RL, *Corsets: A Visual History*, London: R L Shep Publishing, 1993.

SPECIALIST BOOKS

Barthes, R, *The Language of Fashion*, London: Berg Publishers, 2006.

Brewar, F and Gilbert D, *Fashion's World Cities*, London: Berg Publishers, 2006.

Foster, HB, and Johnson D C, *Wedding Dress Across Cultures*, London: Berg Publishers, 2003.

Gale, C and Kaur, J, *Fashion And Textiles: An Overview*, London: Berg Publishing, 2004.

Gere, C, *Digital Culture*, London: Reaktion Books, 2003.

Kawamura, Y, *The Japanese Revolution in Paris Fashion*, London: Berg Publishers, 2004.

Kelley, T and Littman, J, *The Art of Innovation: Lessons in Creativity from IDEO, America's Leading Design Firm*, New York: Doubleday Business, 2001.

Kuchler, S and Miller, D, *Clothing as Material Culture*, London: Berg Publishers, 2005.

Kuniavsky, M, *Observing the User Experience*, London: Morgan Kauffmann, 2003.

Palmer, A and Clark, H, *Old Clothes, New Looks: Secondhand Fashion*, London: Berg Publishers, 2004.

Paulcelli, E, *Fashion Under Fascism: Beyond the Black Shirt*, London: Berg Publishers, 2004.

Quinn, B, *Techno Fashion*, London: Berg Publishers, 2002.

Quinn, B, *The Fashion of Architecture*, London: Berg Publishers, 2003.

Saffer, D, *Designing for Interaction: Creating Smart Applications and Clever Devices*, London: Peachpit Press, 2006.

Troy, N, *Couture Culture*, MIT Press, 2004.

Kawamura Y, *Fashionology: An Introduction to Fashion Studies*, London: Berg Publishers, 2005.

Vinken, B, *Fashion Zeitgeist: Trends And Cycles in the Fashion System*, London: Berg Publishers, 2004.

Welters, L and Cunningham P, *Twentieth Century American Fashion*, London: Berg Publishers, 2005.

Wilson, E, *Adorned In Dreams: Fashion and Modernity*, London: I B Tauris and Co Limited, 2003.

Queen of bohemia, Edie Sedgwick, circa 1960.

ACKNOWLEDGEMENTS

JILL BARRON, BUTTERFLY GIRL, FOR SUPPLYING VINTAGE GARMENTS FOR PHOTOGRAPHING.

APRIL FROM VINTAGE VIXEN FOR COMMENTS REGARDING PURCHASING AND CARE INSTRUCTIONS FOR VINTAGE GARMENTS.

JULIA C QUILLIAM FOR LENDING HER BLACK 1950S EVENING DRESS.

ILLUSTRATOR DAVID REESON, FASHION CONSULTANT TO THE FASHION AND TEXTILE MUSEUM LONDON (NOW PART OF NEWHAM COLLEGE) FOR LIAISING WITH DESIGNERS AND PROVIDING AND SOURCING IMAGERY.

DAVID SASSOON FROM BELLVILLE SASSOON LORCAN MULLANY, BRITISH DESIGNER AND COUTURIER, WHO PROVIDED TIME, IMAGES AND INFORMATION ON THE LAST FOUR DECADES OF THE FASHION INDUSTRY.

ZANDRA RHODES, BRITISH DESIGNER, FOR GENEROUSLY GIVING PERMISSION FOR THE USE OF IMAGES AND FOR LETTING US EXPLORE THE WORKINGS OF HER FASHION STUDIO.

BRIAN KIRKBY AND ZOWIE BROACH FROM BOUDDICCA, FOR THEIR IMAGES AND FOREWORD.

JOAN THORNTON FOR HER KNOWLEDGE ON FASHION DURING THE SECOND WORLD WAR AND FOR SUPPLYING GARMENTS FEATURING THE CC41 LABEL.

IRENE BARNES FOR HER ADVICE AND INFORMATION ON THE EARLY PART OF THE TWENTIETH CENTURY.

SUZANNE POTTS FOR LENDING THE 1960S RICHARD SHOPS DRESS.

HEATHER, RETIRED PATTERN MAKER FOR STYLE SIMPLICITY, FOR HER ADVICE AND INFORMATION ON THE PAPER PATTERN MARKET.

DEREK SEDDON FOR SUPPLYING IMAGES OF VINTAGE CLOTHING.

MINDY, AT FASHION FAIR.

VINTAGE MODES' PATRICK AND SUZI FOR ALLOWING US TO PHOTOGRAPH GARMENTS FROM THEIR STOCK.

EMILIE CLAIBORNE, FINAL YEAR WOMENSWEAR DESIGNER, 2008, RAVENSBOURNE COLLEGE OF DESIGN AND COMMUNICATION.

NIKI PILKINGTON, FASHION PROMOTION STUDENT, RAVENSBOURNE COLLEGE OF DESIGN AND COMMUNICATION, FOR HER ILLUSTRATIONS.

ISABEL WATSON FOR MODELLING GARMENTS.

CATHERINE MALCOLM FOR SUPPLYING VINTAGE ITEMS FOR PHOTOGRAPHING.

DR TUPPY OWENS FOR HER ADVICE AND KNOWLEDGE ON THE LONDON BOUTIQUE CULTURE IN THE 1970S AND HER INPUT ON FASHION AND FETISHWEAR.

VAL FURPHY FOR LENDING COMME DES GARÇONS AND YOHJI YAMAMOTO GARMENTS FROM PERSONAL COLLECTION.

IAIN BROMLEY, VISITING SENIOR LECTURER RAVENSBOURNE COLLEGE OF DESIGN AND COMMUNICATION.

DOROTA WOJCIECHOWSKA, FASHION SUBJECT LEADER BA, COURSE LEADER MA. RAVENSBOURNE COLLEGE OF DESIGN AND COMMUNICATION.

THIS BOOK WOULD NOT HAVE BEEN POSSIBLE WITHOUT:

NADINE MONEM
BLANCHE CRAIG
AARON WALKER
CHARLOTTE CRAIG
ROSIE MCGUINNESS
MARIA BERTRAN
AND THE WONDERFUL NIKOS KOTSOPOULOS.

RAVEN SMITH.

Marks and Spencer skirts from the
1958 Spring/Summer collection.
Courtesy of Marks and Spencer.

© 2008 Black Dog Publishing Limited, London, UK,
the designers and the authors. All rights reserved.

Editor: Raven Smith at Black Dog Publishing
Designer: Josh Baker at Black Dog Publishing

Black Dog Publishing Limited
10A Acton Street
London WC1X 9NG
United Kingdom

info@blackdogonline.com
www.blackdogonline.com

ISBN: 978 1 906155 38 4

British Library Cataloguing-in-Publication Data.

A CIP record for this book is available from the British Library.

Black Dog Publishing Limited, London, UK, is an environmentally
responsible company.

Very Vintage: The Guide to Vintage Patterns and Clothing is printed on IPM Fine
paper, high white woodfree uncoated matt paper, chlorine free, FSC certified.

architecture art design
fashion history photography
theory and things

www.blackdogonline.com